the
secret
message
of
shame

PATHWAYS TO HOPE
AND HEALING

patricia s. potter-efron, m.s., and
ronald t. potter-efron, m.s.w., ph.d.

NEW HARBINGER PUBLICATIONS, INC.

Distributed in the U.S.A. by Publishers Group West; in Canada by Raincoast Books; in Great Britain by Airlift Book Company, Ltd.; in South Africa by Real Books, Ltd.; in Australia by Boobook; and in New Zealand by Tandem Press.

Copyright © 1999 by Ronald T. Potter-Efron and Patricia S. Potter-Efron
New Harbinger Publications, Inc.
5674 Shattuck Avenue
Oakland, CA 94609

Cover design by SHELBY DESIGNS AND ILLUSTRATES
Edited by Carole Honeychurch
Text design by Michele Waters

Library of Congress Catalog Card Number: 99-74372
ISBN 1-57224-170-5 Paperback

New Harbinger Publications' Website address: www.newharbinger.com

01   00   99

10   9   8   7   6   5   4   3   2   1

First printing

Acknowledgments

We want to thank two people in particular. The first is Kristin Beck, without whose perseverance we would never have written this book. Second is Carole Honeychurch, who has been as a thoroughly competent and thoughtful editor.

This book is dedicated to Gail Milgram, Ed.D., Director of the Center for Alcohol Studies at Rutgers University, and to the students and staff of the Rutgers Summer School of Alcohol Studies.

Contents

Preface

Shame: A Message of Hope

Ten years ago we wrote *Letting Go of Shame*, which began with the story of a little girl being told by her mother that she was bad for playing in the mud and having fun. "Shame on you," scolded the mother. The girl immediately felt small, weak, and dirty. As we discovered from reader's responses, there was something very familiar about that little girl. Many people, both men and women, identified with that image of sudden, unanticipated shame. The rest of the book was devoted to describing what shame is, how it develops, and how to heal excessive shame.

   Now, a decade later, we have been given the opportunity to write a second book on shame. The question, of course, is how to improve upon the first. What wasn't said the first time around that might be really important to the reader? We've decided that this book should place more emphasis upon two aspects of shame: 1) the power of hope and optimism when confronting shame; and 2) the effects of shame upon some very common problems in life, such as the way people see themselves, the pressure to conform, self-neglect and self-sabotage, and the formation of addictions.

Why an emphasis upon hope? Because shame is a depressing feeling, a frequently hidden emotion that bursts unbidden into awareness, making people feel utterly hopeless and totally exposed, and then retreating silently into the background of their minds. Shame is quite possibly the hardest emotion to endure personally as well as to work with in therapy. It's even been said that guilt brings people into therapy only for shame to drive them right out again. The merest hint of shame is enough to make some people withdraw from others—and even from themselves. Shame triggers feelings of weakness, helplessness, and hopelessness, often very easily and unexpectedly. Because shame seems so all-encompassing, many people afflicted with it despair, falling into the abyss of hopelessness. Hopelessness is a place of inaction and numbness, where people lose vitality, desire for change, and the ability to think and feel with any richness. Neither survival nor giving up seems to offer relief.

Hope is the antidote for the despair caused by shame. That's why we emphasize hope in the subtitle of this book. Hope. Optimism. Courage. Humor. Finding a way back to faith in oneself. Our goal is to help people understand shame in a newer, more positive manner. Although shame can be a damaging and powerful emotion, learning about shame presents a unique opportunity for positive change, and adding hope into the mix bolsters your powers to fight shame. This combination may even help some readers take control of their emotional lives, even if shame has become dominant.

As we will describe in the text, we're not aiming to eradicate shame. A limited amount of shame has an important place in the sphere of human emotions. Shame is valuable and not damaging as long as it is temporary in length, moderate in intensity, and points people toward what they need to do in order to feel pride and wholeness. Too much shame is the werewolf of emotions, thriving in darkness and secrecy, lunging out of the night to wreak havoc. Excessive shame (what John Bradshaw [1988] calls "toxic shame" or Gershen Kaufman [1996] calls becoming "shame bound") destroys self-esteem. It keeps people from liking themselves, connecting with others, and doing things well. Excessive shame occurs when shame becomes permanent instead of temporary, intense instead of moderate, and points nowhere except into despair. But excessive shame withers in the daylight. Reading this book is part of the illumination process. Our goal is to shed enough light on the subject to help people better understand and manage their lives, including their shame and the ways they participate in increasing it. Our bottom line is that shame is, as they say in some twelve-step programs, "another blankety-blank opportunity to grow."

We've divided this book into two main sections. We describe the core characteristics of shame in the first part: what shame is, how it shows up in people's lives, how people defend against shame, the differences between normal and excessive shame, and, most importantly, the basic ways that people heal their shame. The first section also has chapters on the relationship between shame and healthy pride, how to deal with three separate kinds of shame (about being, belonging, and doing), how shame can actually hint at someone's deepest needs (their yearnings), and creative approaches to handling shame.

The second half of the book is about how shame affects people's daily life. We've selected some common problems for consideration here: the pressure to give up one's uniqueness in order to fit in; why so many men and women in America dislike their bodies and disown their sexuality; how shame and anger combine to form deadly rage; the shame/blame game that ruins so many relationships; shame and the addictive process; and how people with excessive shame harm themselves through acts of self-neglect, self-sabotage, and self-attack. These are painful and difficult topics, to say the least. However, we've made every effort to provide roads out of, as well as into, these discussions. Each chapter offers ways to explore the meanings of these topics in your own life. Some exercises will offer you the added possibility of transforming your shame into mature richness. The paths this book leads to will take you away from the destructiveness of shame and toward hope, pride, optimism, and love. It is our strong conviction that nobody has to live a life of perpetual shame.

—Pat and Ron Potter-Efron

Section I

Core Aspects of Shame

What Is Shame?

1

The Shame Experience

Let's begin with a definition: Shame is "a painful belief in one's basic defectiveness as a human being" (Potter-Efron, Potter-Efron 1989b). Shame is partly pure feeling, partly a set of beliefs. Like all emotions, shame operates on a continuum of intensity from barely noticable experiences to overwhelming ones. People may feel a little shame sometimes, and a lot of shame on other occasions. While a little shame feels mostly embarrassing (as if someone had suddenly swung a spotlight onto you when you had not expected to be noticed), stronger shame experiences often feel humiliating (as if you would rather sink through the floor than still exist, or as if you were entirely worthless).

Here are some of the uncomfortable thoughts and feelings that happen to people during shame episodes. Remember, though, as you read through this list, that only during really bad shame episodes would anyone experience most or all of them. When powerfully shamed, people:

- may not be able to look others in the eye;

- might feel the hot blush of shame on their face;
- could feel totally exposed, as if people could see right through them;
- could judge themselves to be inadequate or defective;
- may feel small and weak;
- may frequently feel judged by others and found to be bad, worthless, incompetent, ugly, dumb or invisible;
- may agree 100 percent with all of those judgments at the time;
- may feel so bad they could think they have no right to anything good;
- may feel exposed and vulnerable, and naturally desire to get away—to withdraw both physically and emotionally;
- right then may not be able to imagine ever again feeling good about themselves;
- may have to struggle against thinking that they're no good, not good enough, unlovable, don't belong, or that they shouldn't exist.

At the most extreme, strongly shamed people may become temporarily suicidal, believing they have no right to exist, or thinking that they would rather die than continue to feel such strong shame. Furthermore, they probably feel isolated and alone, cut off from others, from their spiritual centers, and from themselves. Put simply, people often feel less than fully human during a shame episode.

Over the last couple of decades, many authors have described the shame experience, trying to make sense out of this painful and frequently debilitating emotion. We'd like to summarize some of the most important aspects of shame in the next several pages as well as confront a few misunderstandings that have arisen.

The Core of Shame

Many American writers on shame (starting with Piers and Singer, 1953) believe that the *fear of abandonment* lies at the core of the shame experience. Their reasoning is that shame is the sign of a break in the "interpersonal bridge" the bond of friendship and trust that develops between people when they treat each other with respect (Kaufman 1996). These writers trace the fear of abandonment back to earliest infancy, the time you couldn't survive on your own. The infantile thought process might sound something like: "If I'm not good, Mommy won't love me. If she doesn't love me, she won't feed me. I'd better do whatever she wants and be whoever she wants me to be so she doesn't abandon me." Shame is a sure clue that someone important has seen you and disapproves. That moment of shame can make you change what you're doing, thinking, saying, and feeling. As you get older, the fear of emotional abandonment may become as strong as that of physical abandonment. You probably long for people to be there when you need them. The most healing message anyone could give someone with this kind of fear is that they really want to be with them.

We have noticed two other important fears regularly associated with shame. The first is *the fear of losing yourself.* This represents the flip side of the abandonment issue. Sometimes it seems that you have to abandon yourself, your true or real self, in order to fit in. But then you may experience the shame of being untrue to your own nature. You feel fake, phony, as if you were wearing a mask that you can no longer take off. You can end up treating yourself like an object, a "thing" to be manipulated, an "it." This can lead to bitter feelings of emptiness, personal despair, perhaps suicidality. The message that this kind of shame imparts is that pleasing others is not as important as learning who you are and being faithful to your deeper self. This kind of personal shame reflects a fear that it may be impossible to retrieve your real self if you've abandoned it for too long.

The third shame-related fear is the *fear of incompetence.* People naturally want to do things and do them well. Most people's self-esteem depends upon them taking pride in something they do, whether that's collecting model railroad cars, raising their children, running a company, or building a garage. Shame in this area is quite common in the United States because we are a task and accomplishment oriented society. In an era where everybody is expected to perform and succeed, people fear that they will not be good enough to avoid the shame of comparative failure.

Five Sources of Shame

Where does shame come from? The answer seemed pretty clear a decade ago. Shame was thought almost inevitably to come from a parent's nasty tone of voice, mean words, and possibly excessive physical punishment. Children gradually incorporated the shaming voices of their parents until, finally, they forgot the original source. Although the shaming voices in their heads sounded like they came from themselves, they were really the disguised words of their parents. Personal growth involved disowning those harsh messages while replacing them with more self-affirming ones.

There's no question that one's family of origin can be a major source of internalized messages of shame. Indeed, the therapy we've done with clients often takes exactly the form mentioned above, in which negative messages are replaced with positive ones. However, there are other sources of shame that frequently are as powerful as someone's family of origin.

Adult Shaming Relationships

Marriage. Work. Friendships. Church. These are all areas in which an adult may internalize messages of shame. Sometimes children grow up happily enough, without excessive shame, only to run into situations as adults that generate tremendous amounts of shame. The grouchy spouse who tries to gain power by calling you dumb and lazy. The boss who believes that shaming and intimidation are good ways to get the work done. So called friends who gossip behind your back. Church officials who say you can't be a member of their church because you aren't pure enough. Forget what happened thirty years ago—there's more than enough shame in the present to explain why you feel crumby about yourself. Here's one quick question to ask yourself that taps into this dimension: in the last twenty-four hours, how much praise have you had and how much criticism? How about in the last week? Month? Year?

Social (Group) Shame

Every country has its share of irrational prejudices and biases. In the U.S., shame could start the moment you are born anybody but a heterosexual, white, male Protestant from a comfortably wealthy and intact family of European origin. More shame may develop if you're not athletic, if you're not smart enough or too smart, if you gain weight, or if you start getting too old. This is social shame: an entire segment of the population is looked down upon partly so that others can feel superior. It's very difficult not to absorb this shame, even though it is not really about you. It's all too easy to end up prejudiced against yourself and the groups to which you belong. The prejudice of one woman toward another, one African American toward another, one gay person against another, or one heavy person against another are all examples of group social shame.

Not everyone takes on the shame of their group. Some simply ignore it as much as possible. Others fight back, consciously taking pride in their community or group. Still others convince themselves that their particular group is really better than others instead of worse. They then become contemptuous of those who would hold them in contempt. Needless to add, this way of dealing with group shame only guarantees that group shame will be perpetuated.

Depression

Depression is a common malady, sometimes estimated to strike 10 percent of the population at any time. Some depressions are situational, others biochemical in origin. Biochemical depressions have been linked with the lack of a chemical called serotonin in the brain. This same deficiency is associated with impulsive violence and addiction (Volavka 1995). For many people, biochemical depression also triggers waves of shame, terrible feelings of worthlessness, unlovability, and a sense of their own badness that have nothing to do with reality. This kind of depression related shame normally responds, at least partially, to antidepressant medication.

Self-Shaming

Remember the famous line from the Pogo comic strip: "We have met the enemy, and it is us"? Well, the line for shame could well be: "I have met my shamer, and it is me." Sometimes, even frequently, people can become their own worst enemies. That's when they call themselves terrible names, endlessly compare themselves with others, neglect to take care of themselves because they don't "deserve" it, and treat themselves as objects to be controlled rather than as selves to be cherished. That shame may have sprouted originally in someone else's words or deeds but now they themselves are the ones who keep it growing.

Ultimately self-shame is the thorniest problem for most people. After all, you can separate from family. You can quit a job. You can combat prejudice and get medication for depression. But you can't run away from your own personalized contempt. You must, instead, learn to recognize how you shame yourself and how to turn that process toward self-caring.

You Can Learn How to Live with Shame

Almost everybody feels shame at times. The experience of shame crosses cultural and geographical boundaries. You can recognize the nonverbal signs of shame just about anywhere you could travel. Blush, cover your eyes, and shrink into your body in France, Australia, Japan, or Nigeria and chances are pretty good that others will know you're feeling ashamed. The capacity to feel shame is part of the human condition. Shame only becomes harsher in cultures where it is used as a strong social weapon. It really is unrealistic to set a personal goal of eradicating all of your shame. Shame is just as much a part of you as any other emotion, and you need to try and learn to live with your shame, and to use it to your advantage.

We want to emphasize that people can learn to use shame as a helpful signal rather than as a destructive force in their lives. Shame, once "tamed" by understanding, can be a valuable helper, the kind of friend who tells you what you need to know when you've lost perspective. Shame can even be an experience you can share with understanding and supportive friends. Although shame isn't ever really funny, in retrospect, it can give you both a sense of proportion and of empathy.

The "History" of Shame

In the past, shame was something everyone recognized by feeling but seldom discussed. Then, in 1980s American culture, many people tackled the process of healing many kinds of problems that had been made worse by a deep sense of shame, problems ranging from addiction to alcohol and drugs to eating disorders. People began to talk more openly about shame. The focus was often on people whose lives had been devastated by shame, who felt shame so often and so intensely that almost everything they did at home or work was ruined by shame. Who could blame them for believing that their own shame was their mortal enemy? Shame seemed to be eating them alive from the inside out and all they wanted was to get rid of it for good. John Bradshaw labeled this overwhelming feeling "toxic shame" (1988). Toxic, excessive shame was seen as so damaging that it seemed pretty obvious that it was the enemy and must be destroyed.

There are still many people suffering from toxic shame. You know very well, if you are one of them, that something is terribly wrong in your relationship with shame. But shame is not a microbe or a virus. It's not something foreign that has invaded your soul and must be expelled. Toxic shame is more like an overdose of something necessary to life in small quantities. Carrots provide necessary vitamins, but if carrots are all you eat, you will actually begin to turn orange. Vitamin C is important, but if you ingest too much, you may well get diarrhea. Red and white blood cells are both important to produce, but if you have much too many of either, you will exhibit pronounced signs of serious illness.

Shame is an essential part of your existence. To be human is to feel some shame. That's why it's useless and unreasonable to try to eradicate shame. Think about it this way: No one likes pain, but it can be a very helpful signal. For example, pain will tell you if you are getting burned. Those who no longer have proper pain receptors may get burned, cut, or otherwise hurt without even knowing they are in trouble.

Being able to feel and to recognize pain helps in making safer and more sensible decisions about how to do things. The pain of a cut finger may remind you to use more caution with sharp tools. Being able to feel and to recognize shame is similar to having pain receptors. Being ashamed of what you did when you got drunk may remind you to use more caution with alcohol. Being ashamed of talking behind someone's back may remind you that kindness is a better investment because it won't hurt anybody.

Useful Shame

Shamelessness . . . . . . Useful Shame . . . . . . Toxic Shame

---

THE SHAME CONTINUUM

Think of shame on a continuum. At one end of the scale are those who act shamelessly. These people never blush with shame as they engage in whatever interests them, whether they're hurting other people to get what they want or using their own bodies like garbage dumps. Some of these people are true sociopaths, lacking both shame and guilt. Others are defending against their shame by pretending to be shameless. These people really have so much shame that they can't face it at all.

Those with toxic shame are on the other end of the continuum. These are the people who are plagued with shame that becomes debilitating. Their shame is frequently triggered unintentionally by others making essentially innocent remarks like, "Gee, you look a little tired today. Are you feeling okay?" Furthermore, once their shame has been triggered, they feel completely devastated, overwhelmed with the intensity of the experience. People trapped in toxic shame feel totally defeated by their shame, seeing no way out—no escape from their humiliation.

Useful shame is in the middle of the continuum. Its three main characteristics are that the experiences of shame are temporary, moderate in intensity, and guide people toward ways to feel better about themselves.

Here's an example of useful shame. Two students, named Jerry and Marti, fell in love. As you might expect, they became so engrossed with each other that their studies suffered. One day Jerry had to give an oral report on the history of warfare in the Balkans. He was unprepared. Standing in front of the class, Jerry could feel his face burning with shame. He felt like a fool. On top of that, he received a poor grade for his shabby performance. Now, if Jerry suffered from toxic shame he might have dropped the class or even withdrawn from college after such an embarrassing experience. Instead, he retreated to his room to think things through. He realized that he'd let himself down. He might not be the world's best student, but he had always taken pride in his work. He promised himself to be better prepared in the future, no matter what else was going on in his life. He returned to his studies and made up for his poor grade by writing a good paper on the Balkans. It took a while, but eventually he felt better about himself. He could look once again into a mirror with pride. His shame attack was over, and he actually felt a little pride for dealing with his failure productively.

Useful shame still feels awful. It's not a feeling most people would volunteer for. But useful shame is one of the most valuable emotions. It steers you toward doing the things that will help you feel pride, honor, integrity, and wholeness.

The Useful Functions of Shame

We've just mentioned one value of the shame experience: shame reminds people of what they need to do to feel good about themselves. Normal shame has several other uses as well.

First, shame helps protect your most private, vulnerable self from overexposure (Schneider 1977). Think, for instance, of something about yourself that you would only tell your most trusted friends. Your sexual history. Your deepest dreams. Your most spiritual experience. Good or bad, these private areas are protected by shame. For example, when Sam's friend, Joe, asked him about his love life, Sam's sense of shame warned him against disclosure. "Oh," Sam thought, "Joe wants me to talk with him about my sex life with Jenny. But that's between her and me. She'd never trust me if I told. Besides, I'd feel totally embarrassed. I'd feel ashamed of myself." Sam's sense of shame protects the privacy of two persons. That very shame helps make intimacy possible by protecting what is private and personal from invasion. Without shame, nothing would be special or sacred. Shame helps create a boundary between what is fully open to view and what is personal.

Secondly, the anticipation of shame protects you from your own inappropriate or excessive drives, wants, and needs. Anticipatory shame produces "I want _____ but not here or now or too much" thoughts. Useful shame helps keep you from eating all seven doughnuts on the tray or from making sexual advances to your best friend's spouse. Useful shame acts as a sensible voice of moderation and morality.

Finally, normal shame reveals you to yourself. Shame helps people realize who they are and who they aren't. The shame message here is not about good or bad but about personal integrity: "No, that's not who I am. I'd feel ashamed of myself if I _____" Shame helps each person answer the intriguing questions, "Who am I?" and "Who am I becoming?"

Psychological Defenses Against Shame

Shame hurts. Sometimes it stings so badly that people can't stand it. That's when they develop psychological defenses that buffer against that pain.

Denial is the most basic psychological defense against shame. "No, this isn't happening. I don't feel bad. I won't feel shame." People in denial refuse to accept their shame by refusing to accept reality. They close their eyes to what is really happening, hoping that the shame hanging around will be gone when they open their eyes again.

Withdrawal is probably the most common defense against shame. Running away. Avoiding others. Staying alone at home where you feel safe. People who use this defense often have been badly shamed in the past. They've learned to fear the possibility of more humiliation. They retreat at the merest hint of criticism or disapproval. They take the position that, "No one can make me feel more shame if I'm not even there and they can't find me."

Perfectionism is another defense against shame. Perfectionists dread making any mistakes because anything less than perfect is shameful. They try to stay one step ahead of their shame by doing everything exactly right (and by not even trying to do something that they might not do perfectly). In a tight corner, they may procrastinate so that if what they do isn't perfect, it's only because they "just didn't have time."

Shaming others is a fourth defense. People who do this often use sarcasm, contempt, and direct shaming attacks ("put-downs") to make others feel ashamed. They try to keep others looking at their own faults so no one will see theirs. They feel better by making others feel worse. They can only feel unashamed when the focus is on other people's mistakes or shortcomings.

Seeking power and control over others is another method for defending against the feelings of weakness and ineffectiveness that shame brings with it. People who are feeling ashamed lose a sense of personal power, as if they no longer were in complete control of their own bodies and minds. One way to try to combat this internal weakness is to try to get power over others. It's almost as if they said to themselves "Well, I feel empty and vulnerable inside. Out of control. I'd better control others so nobody will see my weakness." This need to gain power over others never really fixes the inner shame, though, because all the power in the world over others doesn't give people power over themselves.

A sixth defense against shame is *arrogance*. Shame often makes a person feel very small. With arrogance, people puff themselves up to resist the feeling of being small that is so much a part of the shame experience. They act like they're bigger than anyone else. They try to convince themselves that they're special, superior, better than everybody—but all the while they secretly believe they're just the opposite: small, shameful, inferior, worthless.

Earlier, we mentioned the seventh defense against shame called *shamelessness*. Here, people turn shame on its head, showing off what shames them in an effort to normalize it. At the same time, they are desperate to hide the core of the problem. They might, for instance, parade around in very revealing outfits that seem to say they have no bodily shame while their appearance or sexuality is something they are actually very uncomfortable about. They might see promiscuity as a way to "prove" that they don't have any sexual problems, or drink everyone "under the table" in order to prove they don't have a problem with alcohol. (The truth is, this last example is a sign of increased tolerance and perhaps addiction.)

Rage is the last common defense against shame. "Ragers" basically attack anybody who conceivably might try to shame them, which of course could mean just about everyone in the world. Their message is crude and simple: "You'll be sorry if you touch my shame!" Rage like this is associated with violence, both verbal and physical.

Human beings use defenses to avoid pain and discomfort. For example, you may lie to others about something shameful so they won't find out you embarrassing secrets. Even worse, though, you may tell lies to yourself so you don't have to deal with your shame. People lie to themselves when they are so ashamed of a possibility or reality that they refuse to even consider whether it might be true or not. For example, if you believe that sword swallowers are morally bad, crazy, and undisciplined people who just want attention and refuse to do any real work for a living, you will probably deny being a sword swallower to yourself, even if you *have* "experimented" with sword swallowing. Lying to yourself makes it possible to deny to yourself who you really are—so, because you would *never* be a sword swallower, you certainly don't have to be ashamed.

On the other hand, if sword swallowing is just another potential health problem and you believe no one needs to be ashamed about health issues, you might feel free to find out if your experimentation with sword swallowing has caused any physical damage, or if it is just a fun hobby. It's easier to ask questions and to get information when you aren't afraid of shame.

People need their defenses. Without them, they might have a hard time functioning at all. However, in the long run, the best way to deal with shame is to face it head on. People need to learn what their shame feels like, how and when it's triggered, and how to get through this very painful feeling. You need the courage to recognize how you defend against shame so that you can begin to lay those defenses aside.

Healing Shame

In *Letting Go of Shame*, we described a two stage healing process for shame: understanding and action. We've modified that process a little over the years, but the basic goals remain the same. The first goal is to understand your own unique relationship with shame. The second is to change that relationship as needed, especially if toxic shame has come to dominate your life.

You'll need to be patient, curious, and accepting to get through the understanding phase. Patience is especially critical because shame is the most hidden of emotions.

Pat Potter-Efron once asked a deeply shamed client to go home and spend a week walking through the woods. She asked him only to think about one question: "How do oak trees grow?" His answer was quite profound: "They grow slowly." Well, shame heals as slowly as oak trees grow. But grow they must. Heal you must. You can heal excessive shame if you are patient and give yourself plenty of time.

Letting yourself be curious about your shame is another aspect of the understanding phase. These are some of the questions you'll need to ask:

- When do I feel shame? What triggers my shame?
- Where in my body do I feel shame?
- How do I defend against shame?
- Where has my shame come from?
- What's keeping me right now from feeling pride, wholeness, self-worth?
- How is my shame affecting my connections with my family, at work, and with others?
- Which common shame messages (I'm no good, I'm not good enough, I'm unlovable, I don't belong, and I shouldn't exist) most affect me?

Finding your own personal answers to these questions brings shame out of hiding. Even if you think of shame as a monster, certainly it's better to face that monster head on than not know where it might strike. Letting yourself be curious about your shame usually "demonsterizes" it, making the shame less threatening, less powerful. There's a tremendous difference between, "Oh, I know what's happening now. That's my shame trying to make me screw up again," and, "I don't know what's happening to me but I know it's something awful."

Acceptance is the third main tool you'll need for the understanding phase. Self-acceptance. Acceptance of reality. Most of all, acceptance of shame as part of the human condition. People must accept their shame before they can change it, but a simple sense of acceptance begins to change their relationship with shame. Shame is no longer the enemy, something to be eradicated and fought. Instead, it is part of you, just as important as your other emotions such as joy, anger, and fear.

Patience, curiosity, and acceptance are the specific uncovering tools people need in the understanding phase. In the action phase, you will also need personal responsibility, planning, and perseverance.

Personal responsibility is the cornerstone for change. Taking responsibility for your shame might be summed up in the statement, "Now that I understand my shame I realize that only I can change it." This is particularly true for self-shaming episodes, the kind where the only person attacking you is yourself. Even when others are trying to shame you, your responsibility extends only to your own behavior. Just because someone says something shaming doesn't mean you have to absorb that shame. Instead, you can recognize it for what it is and decline to take it in. Taking personal responsibility for your shame is the opposite of uselessly blaming others for your misery. Shame simply cannot heal without your willingness to be the guide for your own life.

Taking personal responsibility demands courage. It takes courage to change because change involves disruption, giving up the known (even if what's familiar is bad) for the unknown. Of course, it helps to have a general road map on your journey from shame toward pride, but nobody can predict the exact travel route.

With shame, you must ask yourself difficult questions, such as, "What am I doing that adds to my shame?" Healing shame goes beyond just asking tough questions, though. It means challenging yourself to change the very ways you think about and treat yourself. That's where conscious planning is vital to healing shame. Each person needs to develop a workable plan that addresses every major source of shame in their lives. Each plan will be different, of course.

Perseverance is as necessary to action as patience is to understanding. People don't simply quit shaming themselves overnight. It takes time. Also, there will certainly be disappointments along the path, perhaps occasions when your shame resurfaces in full strength. It's important to keep going during these times, and not to feel totally defeated by shame.

Shame can be healed through understanding and action. Excessive shame can be reduced to normal levels. Self-hatred can be transformed into self-love. That is the message of hope that lies at the core of this book. Healing shame means using the opportunity to grow that you are offered.

If you are ready to face, demystify, and reduce your shame, you will need a few ground rules to follow. Here are a few basic ones, along with a few suggestions that can make the process simpler and easier.

Ground Rules for Handling Stress

1. Look at the sources of your shame, not away from them. People who use compulsive means of escaping can't see themselves clearly. People who are busy criticizing others can't see themselves very well, either. They're looking in the wrong direction. Do your best to get a good look at the sources and reasons for the shame that bothers you.

2. Don't blame others for your feelings. True, there may be people in your life who are critical of you or seem to think you are incompetent. They reinforce your worst fears about yourself. But you have a responsibility to decide what is right for you, and as you work on your own shame, you'll find that you do not always agree with those people. Recognize that shaming them back won't be very helpful, and that you can be in charge of the things about yourself which you believe and accept. Separate their old business from your own and remind yourself that you will be getting stronger. Taking this responsibility will move you closer to the place where you are in charge of how you use all your emotions and ideas, putting them to work toward the betterment of your life.

3. Don't assume that something is bad because you feel ashamed of it. Some good things you may have learned to be ashamed of are recognizing your own needs, expressing love, taking care of yourself, standing up for what you believe is right, or having fun. These aren't automatically bad things. Consider whether your shame is excessive.

4. Look for any immediate message your shame may be giving you. Ask yourself if the messages you're getting from shame are accurate, and if so, how you could change your behavior to feel better about yourself. If you feel bad about being lazy and have been watching TV eight hours a day, you can probably think of some ways to improve your emotional

state. However, if you are feeling ashamed of being lazy because you're taking a break after several hours of work, you need to try to talk back to your shame more convincingly (which you'll learn about later in the book).

5. Know in advance that there will be times you will feel uncomfortable and feel as if your shame will never end. It *will* end, and you *can* get through it. In order to let go of a pattern of behavior or emotion, you need to take a good look at it. That means that in order to let go of shame, you must look at it, understand it, and make a conscious decision about it. You may feel terrible while you're taking your shame out to the trash can. If you can leave it there for at least a while, however, you will begin to feel a whole lot better.

6. Have some kind of backup available. That means both someone you will be able to talk to if necessary, and a list of ten (or twenty!) positive things you can go do when shame threatens to take over. Put the following kinds of things on your list:
   · things you usually like to do;
   · things that give you a sense of hope;
   · things that are creative;
   · things that help you relax;
   · things that take you into safe, natural settings.

7. While you are working through your shame, don't drink very much or very often, and use any unprescribed drugs in moderation because they will distort how you feel. Whether they increase or decrease your shame on a temporary basis, they prevent you from thinking clearly and from getting deep enough into your thoughts and feelings to sense the positive yearnings that may be wrapped inside the shame.

Some Additional Suggestions

• Self-respect comes in part from respecting others, so don't let anger take over. If you feel anger overcoming you and need a time out, take one.

• Be creative. Whether you try writing, drawing, storytelling, painting, carving, woodworking, or sewing, let what you do speak to you. Your inner self is wiser than you can imagine. You will discover that you're surprising and essentially lovable.

- Cherish your differences. Enjoy the ways in which you are uniquely yourself. Consider the aspects of the groups to which you belong that are special and positive. Find ways to take pride in yourself as someone who is different and unique.

- Don't abandon yourself. By that we mean you need to trust and respect yourself even when others are critical or shaming you. You'll be much less afraid of the abandonment of others if you know that you can and will "be there" for yourself.

- Remember that you are an adult. You are who you are, and you can't be swallowed up by another human being. Whenever you begin to feel as if you might lose yourself, remember that you have your own body, brain, and experiences.

- Share safely. Don't share shame issues with people who will only shame you more or use what you share as a weapon later. Try to find people who will listen, instead of telling you what to do (even if you want them to just tell you what to do). Talk with people who encourage you in positive ways. And remember that no one completely understands another person. Two people can think and feel differently without either one of them having to be ashamed.

Exercises

We believe these exercises will help you learn more about how the material in this book applies personally to you. But, before beginning, please remember what we said in the preface: these exercises are for you to use as you wish. There are no right or wrong answers, no expectations about what you should say, write, or do. We do suggest taking your time and using a notebook or journal but these are optional.

1. Think of a time when physical pain gave you a message you needed to hear about self-caring, and you used that message to help yourself. Now think of a time when your shame told you that you had done something wrong that could hurt you. Did you use that message to help yourself? How? If you did not use that message to help yourself, do you still feel that old shame still hanging around? What behavior would you have to engage in to let the "inner you" know that you've gotten that message?

2. Here is a list of commonly held values. Rank them on the left side according to what is most important to you (#1 is tops). When you have finished, rank them again on the right side, according to the ones you would feel the most ashamed about violating (#1) to least ashamed.

   Are your lists similar or inconsistent? If they really don't seem to match, you may have acquired toxic shame in some areas, or you may not know yourself as well as you think you do.

   _____ responsible _____

   _____ compassionate _____

   _____ independent _____

   _____ trustworthy _____

   _____ honest _____

   _____ fair _____

   _____ hard-working _____

   _____ moral _____

   _____ frugal _____

   _____ cooperative ____

3. Find a notebook you can use as a journal. Enter any thoughts, feelings, drawings, or experiences that lead you to feel empty, no good, not good enough, not lovable, like you don't belong, or like you should not exist. Let yourself argue with these perceptions. For example, "Mary said she didn't feel good enough as a teacher, but I think she is. I feel like I'm not good enough a lot. But *feeling* not good enough isn't the same thing as *being* not good enough. Mary is harder on herself than she would be on another teacher. Maybe I'm harder on myself than on others, too. When I'm feeling 'not good enough' that may simply mean that I can't see myself very well right then." Or: "Jeff said no one else would ever want me, I'm so ugly. Sometimes I feel like that is true. When he says that, he is talking ugly himself. Maybe he is being mean because he is afraid I might not want him. It's important to question the motives of people who shame others the way he shames me." As you get better at arguing with these feelings, you will be discovering that there really is an alternative to shaming yourself or tolerating shaming yourself on an everyday basis.

4. Choose one of the following sayings—or a favorite of your own—to write down and carry in your wallet or purse. Read it over several times a day.

a) Blessed are those who can laugh at themselves, for they shall be eternally amused. —Anonymous

b) If you are patient enough, even an egg will walk. —Nigerian proverb

c) The deeper sorrow carves into your being, the more joy you can contain. —Kahlil Gibran

d) Everywhere hands lie open to catch us as we fall. —Anonymous

e) The moon is not shamed by the barking of dogs. —Southwest Native American proverb

f) No one else can represent your conscience. —Ashinabe proverb

What Is the Opposite of Shame?

Shame Is Self-Conscious Judgment

Shame is far more than a pure physical sensation. Indeed, we defined shame in the first chapter as a painful belief in one's defectiveness as a human being. That definition emphasizes the perhaps uniquely human ability to watch yourself as you work, play, and interact. People observe themselves—and then judge their actions. People feel shame when they judge themselves as somehow failing in those actions. They're not good enough, smart enough, attractive enough, and so on. Something about them is inadequate. They then feel shameful—literally full of shame.

Shame, then, is a self-conscious emotion, a judgment of the self by the self. But this judgment doesn't remain simply a negative feeling about yourself, an abstract, undefined sense that you have. Shame is quickly translated from feelings into words. Over the years, people have developed a shame vocabulary, a collection of crude and subtle words that forcefully convey self-criticism. Here are some: "I am . . . defective, dirty, an embarrassment, ugly, stupid, evil, horrible, worthless, pitiful, weak, useless." Each word speaks to some part of the shame experience. But each word is a little different from the rest. Also, each word might mean something different to different people. With regards to shame, then, you may become a veritable poet of despair, creating and collecting the words and phrases with which you judge yourself as shameful.

But, if you'd like to remove your poet's mantle and choose to forego shame, what is your alternative: What is the opposite of shame? Is it simply a neutral state, so that either you feel shame or you don't? Or might there be something positive to aim for, more or less the flip side of the shame experience? This is actually a critical question because the answer determines one's goals in the area of shame. If there is no positive goal, then the best you can hope for is to eliminate shame. As noted in chapter 1, getting rid of one's shame was indeed the main goal when shame was first written about in the late 1980s. Shame was conceived of as a negative, damaging emotion that needed to be eliminated. But what if you could identify a more positive goal than simply eradicating shame? Then the very effort of studying this painful feeling would be much more worthwhile. Your shame could begin becoming transformed into . . . what?

Pride

Just as the word "shame" actually represents a cluster of negative, self-judging terms, so we need one word that can serve as shame's opposite. That word, we submit, is "pride." The concept of pride implies positive judgments about the self. True, people who have pride still observe and judge themselves, but for them the thumbs go up instead of down. "I am good enough. I am lovable. I do belong. I'm okay." Pride is shorthand for an entire cluster of words, as we shall soon describe, with which you can judge yourself to be at the very least adequate and sometimes superior.

Here's our definition of *pride*: a positive belief in one's basic worthiness as a human being.

Before continuing, let us distinguish the pride we're describing from what is sometimes called "foolish pride," "arrogance," "false pride," or "grandiosity." These are all states of *excessive* pride, usually unearned. In other words, people feel false pride when they think they are better than others or when they have overinflated notions of their importance. Arrogance like this is actually a defense against shame, someone's attempt to convince themselves that they are really something when deep down they feel totally empty and worthless. This grandiosity must be confronted by the arrogant person facing their shame. Only when the too proud individual recognizes that their life has been a balloon full of hot air can that person learn how to be real. Sometimes egos have to be deflated and humility learned.

But the pride we are describing is earned and real. It's an acknowledgment by the self to the self that, "Yes, I am good enough. I am worthy. I am competent." It's the legitimate pride people take when they've done something well, when they've shown caring and love to their children or partner, when they are at peace with themselves at the end of the day. This is not a comparative pride. It's not "I'm good because I'm better than Joe or Mary or Pat." It's the quiet satisfaction that comes with knowing that you're making a valuable contribution to the world.

Here's the kind of pride we're talking about. Ron studied sociology at Purdue University. His major professor there, Walter Hirsch, had a phrase that we feel reflects this sort of honest pride: "We are all laborers in the vineyards of knowledge." By that we think he meant that each person has a job to do but that no single job is more or less important than another's. And just as you are a laborer in the vinyards of knowledge, so you are a laborer in the vinyards of life. Your job is to nurture the vines around you as best you can, to do more good than harm, and to notice and acknowledge your real but limited contribution to the universe. That is real pride.

The Circle of Pride

Just as no one word explains the entire shame experience, there are a large cluster of words that describe pride. Each word says something a little different about pride. In addition, each word represents a goal or a direction. The road map that leads to pride is full of the words listed in figure 1: autonomy, strength, vigor, competence, purpose, respect, dignity, humility, acceptance, wholeness, and integrity. None of these words stands completely alone, of course. Any experience that contributes to someone's sense of personal integrity, for instance, may very well also help that person feel more competent, dignified, and invigorated. Each connotes the other, but, at the same time, they are distinct. Most important, every experience someone has of any of these terms leads them toward the center of the circle, toward pride.

Independence

Integrity   Strength

Wholeness   Vigor

Acceptance   **Pride**   Competence

Humility   Purpose

Dignity   Honor

Respect

Figure 1. THE CIRCLE OF PRIDE

Please note that the twelve words arranged in the compass of pride have an order. The four main compass point words set at what would be north, east, south, and west (independence, competence, respect, and acceptance) represent what we believe are the four most critical aspects of pride, especially for those who are in the process of dealing with shame issues. The words between north and east (strength and vigor) describe mixtures of autonomy and competence; the words between east and south (purpose and honor) combine competence and respect, and so on, around the circle.

Let's try to describe these words in greater detail now, in particular the four main compass-point words. We choose to begin with "respect," since learning to respect yourself is so important for those who want to reduce the power of shame over their lives.

Respect

Dictionary definitions of respect vary, but most highlight the idea that respect involves valuing a person both for who they are and for what they do. To respect someone is to admire them, even to defer to them because of their knowledge or wisdom. You "show respect" to those you have respect for by listening to them, taking their ideas seriously, and in general by refraining from attacking or shaming them.

You may be wondering if we're referring to self-respect or respecting others. The answer is *both*, since one leads to the other when you truly believe that there is enough goodness to go around in this world. In our counseling practice and other writings we stress the need to quit shaming and start respecting others if you want to feel better about yourself (see *I Deserve Respect*, 1989). But here we want to focus on self-respect.

What does it mean really to respect yourself? Minimally, self-respectful behavior precludes self-shaming and self-attack. Nobody demonstrates respect by calling somebody, including yourself, nasty names. Self-respect means treating yourself as politely as you would someone you admire. In addition, self-respect means noticing your positive qualities—those things about yourself that you value the most—and nurturing them. Thirdly, since you probably respect those with wisdom, you would also learn to listen to your intuitive wisdom figure, the part of you that seems to sense the truth about important matters. A person's intuitive wisdom figure is like a bloodhound on the trail of goodness. It can sniff out the right way to go even when everything seems hopelessly confused. It's also a good "B.S. detector," in that your intuitive wisdom figure is pretty good at turning away from advice that just doesn't smell quite right.

In order to heal excessive shame, one critical question you can ask yourself every day is this: "How can I respect myself today?" Take the time to listen for a positive answer (not something like "Just don't do anything stupid," which is really a disrespectful rebuke but a message more like, "Take enough pride in the good ideas you have today to follow up on them").

Acceptance

"I am not acceptable," is one of shame's strongest messages. For some, that means that they aren't acceptable at that moment because of something particular they're doing. For others, the phrase, "I am not acceptable," is followed by the word "ever." These shame-bound people think they are lost causes—so fatally flawed that they are beyond repair.

The question you may want to ask in response to this kind of statement is, "Not acceptable to whom?" To your parents? Your spouse? Your friends? Your boss? The world? All of these people's opinions matter a lot. In fact, because of an instinctive fear of abandonment, people learn to conform to other people's expectations for them. You naturally fear being considered unacceptable and do what you can to comply. Moments of shame can frequently be translated as, "Now look what you've done. People won't like that. They won't like you. You'd better stop doing that right now. That's unacceptable behavior." Unfortunately, it's easy to go from discovering that what you do is unacceptable to believing that who you *are* is also unacceptable. Even worse, you can internalize the sense of unworthiness. Then you become unacceptable even to yourself. That's when shame takes up permanent residence in your brain. Self-rejecting, you think you're so bad that nobody, especially including yourself, would want to get to know you.

What's essential to healing shame is to become more self-accepting. That involves two main processes. First, shameful folks need to deal with the dread of abandonment that makes them desperately conform. Secondly, they must forgive themselves for being human and therefore flawed.

There's a difference between the child's and adult's fear of abandonment. Only the child need fear death through abandonment. So, as an adult, one way toward self-acceptance is to remember that you can survive rejection. True, rejection hurts. Certainly abandonment would wound you. But as an adult you can and will survive even in the face of abandonment and rejection. That reality means you can sometimes choose to stand alone, to say or do something disapproved of by others. Another way to put it is this: "Just because you reject me doesn't mean I have to reject myself. Now I know your disapproval won't kill me."

Self-forgiveness is another way to become more self-accepting. Self-forgiving persons realize they'll inevitably screw up because screwing up is part of the human condition. They are flawed, limited, imperfect. Even as they strive to correct their shortcomings, though, they understand that nobody's perfect. They forgive themselves for their ineptitude, work around their weaknesses, and maintain a good sense of humor that they can implement when they realize that they may be taking themselves too seriously. The great wisdom about self-acceptance they have discovered is that it's possible to love yourself for who you are while still working to improve.

Independence

Shame-bound people often believe they have little control over their own lives. Their shame has left them feeling weak and inept.

Instead of feeling like a pilot guiding the ship of their lives, they feel more like a leaf floating helplessly on the water. That makes them terribly dependent upon others. They may very well resent how easily they are blown around, but they have lost faith in their ability to think and choose. This sense of helplessness is a sure sign of excessive shame.

Independence is the antidote for feeling out of control. That means taking responsibility for your own life without trying to control anybody else. It means developing a strong faith in your own ability that actually helps you work interdependently with others. Independence also involves taking pride in your ability to make your own decisions.

We want to emphasize that we're not talking about a "You can't make me" sense of independence. That's actually counter-dependence, a desperate rejection of other's wishes. The kind of independence that leads to pride is more positive than that. It answers the question, "What do I want to say yes to? What's really important to me?"

Competence

Competence is the fourth compass point in the circle of pride. Here we stress something often forgotten in the literature on self-esteem, namely that self-worth must be based in real effort and accomplishment.

It's not only that deeply shamed people often feel inadequate. The problem is that their shame has helped make them incompetent as well. For instance, someone who avoids public speaking because of the fear of humiliation may very well speak poorly in public because of both lack of competence and lack of practice. Avoidance leads to incompetence that produces more avoidance in a doomsday spiral. Shame begets shame.

Fortunately, this spiral can be reversed. We've seen hundreds of people who've moved from shame to pride. Almost without exception, these people have discovered that they are far more skillful than they ever thought. But these skills don't spring up like crocuses on the first warm day of spring. They need to be nurtured and developed.

Here's an example. Sandra is about thirty-five years old. She's been hurt badly and repeatedly in her life, so much so that she pretty much retreated to her home. There she mostly stared at the walls and frightened herself with memories from the past. She also convinced herself she'd never be good at anything. Sandra was especially certain that she could never meet people, work a job, or develop a relationship. Over the years she did indeed regularly fail at all of these endeavors, each episode further convincing her of her basic worthlessness. But then Sandra started working on her shame concerns. She gradually began challenging her built-in sense of incompetence. She started venturing out of her house, at first just to see if she could survive. Over a period of a couple years, Sandra gained confidence and competence. Eventually she found a part-time job that she not only could keep but could do well. She made real friends. She even found a nonabusive boy friend who treats her with respect. Gradually pride is displacing shame in Sandra's life, confidence and competence replacing shame and failure.

Respect, acceptance, independence, and competence are the four major compass points on the circle of pride. But in between these points are other, equally valuable concepts.

Dignity

Self-respect sometimes shows up in the way people walk and talk. People with a sense of dignity tend to "walk tall." That is, they stride forward with confident steps, unstooped, eyes forward, unafraid, and unashamed. They fill the space around them. The message they convey is that they are sure of themselves, even that they take pride in themselves. However, they don't strut or look affected (that would be false dignity). They aren't trying to look better than others.

Contrast this dignified manner with the demeanor of shame. Shame forces one's eyes down. People don't stride in shame—they shuffle while they seem to shrink into themselves. Shamed people tend to make weak gestures, keeping their limbs close to their bodies, in a sign of diffidence.

Certainly nonverbal mannerisms can be faked. The apparently confident person may really be a quivering mass of Jell-O inside. On the other hand, learning to walk without shame might help someone develop greater self-confidence so that they actually begin to feel better about themselves.

The idea of dignity, though, addresses more than mere appearance. People frequently use the phrase "quiet dignity" to refer to someone they respect, particularly someone whose sense of worthiness comes from inside and so doesn't have to be visibly exhibited. These calmly dignified persons have the ability not to panic when others are shaken, not to gossip when others tell stories, not to feel good at the expense of others. People believe they can learn from such individuals—not only specific pieces of information, but how to live a personally fulfilling life.

Humility

Shame lives on a vertical line. By that we mean shame thrives when people constantly compare themselves to each other. Who is better? Worse? At what? When? How? The most obviously shamed people always lose when they make comparisons. They think they are that much worse than others. But what about the people who think they always win? Doesn't their sense of superiority often mask their own battles with shame? Why, if they feel so confident about themselves, do they have to keep trying to prove their superiority?

The mere act of comparing usually increases the potential for shame. That's why even the "A" student at school, the "perfect 10" gymnast, and the thin-as-paper model might still feel dumb, clumsy, or heavy. No matter how successful, they have become consumed by the process of comparing themselves with others. Inevitably someone will appear who is just a little smarter, more graceful, or thinner. While the act of comparison is sometimes useful, it is critical to be able to quit comparing in order to lessen the potential for shame. That's where the concept of humility comes in.

The principle of humility is this: no person is intrinsically better or worse than any other. Certainly everybody has unique gifts and virtues. Some are more gifted than others. But at a deeper level, at the level of core humanity, people are far more alike than different.

The journey from shame to pride often involves stepping off the ladder of comparison. It means declining invitations to feel better or worse than others. It also means looking for that which connects you with others rather than that which sets you apart. True humility connects us with all that is common among humankind.

Honor

Honor connotes an adherence to principle. Honorable persons are honest, fair, and loyal to their beliefs. Their behavior is credible and moral. Honor is a distinction won over time. Although people are sometimes honored for a single, courageous act (the Medal of Honor) more often they are recognized for a long career of responsible and distinguished deeds.

How does honor relate to shame? Well, think of what it means to be dishonorable. People commit dishonorable acts when they do things that are untrue to themselves or society. Dishonorable behavior brings shame to the person who does it. By contrast, honorable actions help people feel healthy pride.

Honor is not all about society's judgment. At a more profound level, you must find ways to honor yourself in daily activity. That means carefully examining your daily routines and actions. Will what I do today help me take pride in myself? To begin trying to bring more honor into your life, you might begin by asking yourself these questions: "Will I be honoring my core beliefs and values? Or will I bring dishonor to myself? If so, perhaps I need to change."

Purpose

People strive to put purpose and meaning into their lives. But, as Gershen Kaufman notes, sometimes significant others such as parents and partners may scoff at your goals (1996). For example, what happens to the child who tells their parents they want to be a farmer only to hear them say that they've worked far too hard in life for one of their kids to have to work with their hands? What happens to the would-be artist told by their spouse that art is a waste of time and so, no, they can't put any art supplies into the budget? Quite possibly these people's purpose becomes shame bound. They feel bad about even wanting to farm or paint. They may even feel shame about wanting any meaning in their lives. Eventually they turn away from what would have given their lives purpose, perhaps eventually forgetting that once they dreamed of something great. They get busy, too busy to tune in on the radio of their dreams. Even if they did try to find their station, their shame would produce so much static that no meaning and purpose messages could get through.

People gain a sense of pride when they discover or reconnect with that which gives their lives meaning and purpose. There's something special when you're doing those things, whether they are farming, painting, praying, or accounting. Furthermore, you must be deeply connected with yourself to discover what really matters to you. One of the great gifts that comes from working through one's shame is the discovery of personal goals that add meaning to life.

Vigor and Strength

Vigor and strength are placed in the circle between independence and competence. That's because positive energy is essential to make and implement independent choices. Actually, these two aspects of pride could be lumped together under the term "vitality." Just as excessive shame drains people of energy so does pride increase their vigor. While shame saps people of their strength, pride helps them feel powerful both physically and emotionally. As excessive shame decreases, people often discover that what they thought were symptoms of clinical depression—lack of energy, lethargy, boredom—was actually caused by their shame. Too much shame is depressing in all the senses of that word.

Pride doesn't just happen. People with pride are usually active, busy at meaningful work, energetic. They take pride in their contributions to the world. They feel personally empowered, strong, alive. They are invigorated with the excitement of life itself.

Integrity

Integrity means being completely honest with yourself and following through on your beliefs. When someone says, "I have to be true to myself. To do that I need to take some time to think about what I really want," that represents a quest for personal integrity. Honesty like this increases a person's self-respect and leads toward healthy pride. People with personal integrity seldom give in to the pressure to conform if that entails being dishonest to themselves. In that sense they resist social shame in order to preserve their personal worth.

Wholeness

Wholeness is the final outcome of the movement toward pride. Where shame disrupts and splits the self, pride reconnects and joins. The result is a complete human being, someone whose day-to-day actions, thoughts, and feelings reflect joy in life, spiritual awareness, celebration of others, and positive well-being. This person has a place in the universe, a reason for being.

Wholeness permits flexibility. People can sense their own multiplicities and contradictions without having to judge and decide amongst them. Thus, they can play or work, be serious or silly, watch a movie or pray, eat sparingly or indulge. They can do all of the above because they are all these things. They do not have to renounce aspects of themselves that once might have been unacceptable to others. They live not to avoid shame and rejection but to embrace all of life.

Exercises

1. Let's take a look at the opposite of the shame experience. If you choose opposite characteristics for the person who has the experience of "non-shame," we find a person who:

   - can look others in the eye;
   - feels there is something right about who they are;
   - judges themselves to be adequate and effective;
   - feels "as big as life";
   - may feel judged by others as good, worthwhile, competent, good-looking, smart;
   - may agree 100 percent with those judgments;
   - knows they have a right to good things;
   - doesn't feel the need to withdraw or avoid;
   - knows they can feel good about themselves and does;
   - knows that as a human being they are good, good enough, lovable, belong in the world, and that it's good that they exist;
   - knows even if they are alone and isolated that they are in touch with others, with their spiritual center, and with themselves;
   - knows they are fully human, and that being human is all right.

   If you were having *this* kind of an experience, what would you call it (no sarcasm allowed)? Would it feel neutral or positive? What would you be inclined to call it: pride, self-respect, competence, acceptance, wholeness, or one of the other words in the "circle of pride" on page 28? Which word would describe this experience best for you? Even if shame has become a big part of your life, one or more of those words can trigger your recognition. Everyone has had some successes in life and can recognize what it's like to feel better about ourselves.

   What are the things in your experience that have led to feeling the opposite of shame in the past? Write them in your journal, and notice the characteristics of the experiences that gave you better feelings about yourself. Which ones were about who you are? Which were about how you belong? Which have to do with things you have done? Could any of those particular kinds of experiences help you feel better about yourself right now?

2. Without being destructive in any way, find an unusual place to write "I deserve respect," and put it somewhere where it will come to your attention regularly. If possible, explore the idea of writing it several times in several different places. For example, Pat noticed that she could put it on the refrigerator in magnetic letters, paste it inside the cookie jar cover, write it in the dust on the top of the TV set, write it in soap on the bathroom mirror, put it on little slips of paper and put one in each dresser drawer, stick one in her slipper for later, paint it on the cow's fence, send it to herself in a letter, write it with the stones in her flower bed, and stitch it and hang it on the wall. She thought of using only those letters for alphabet soup, but decided that was too much work, because it would be too hard to read. We are sure that you can come up with some ideas that we haven't. After you have written "I deserve respect" somewhere unusual, check once a day to make sure it is still there. When you get tired of it there, or someone else removes it, try another spot where you're sure to find it. Keep it around you until you are absolutely sure that it's true.

3. Rate the following statements, "T" if mostly true or "F" if mostly false. Over time, go back over this list and underline each statement as it becomes true for you in any situation, and remember to write that incident in your journal.

Respect:

_____ I am valuable just because I am myself. No one else sees the world in quite the same way I do.

_____ I notice what I like about myself, and encourage myself to continue to be that way.

_____ When things seem very confusing, I really listen for the wise part inside of me.

Acceptance:

_____ I can accept myself even when I'm not so happy with what is happening in my life.

_____ Even though it's sometimes hard, I refuse to abandon myself and what I know is best for me in order to please others.

_____ I can and do forgive myself for my mistakes.

Independence:

_____ I make the decisions about my own life instead of asking or manipulating others to make decisions for me.

____ Being responsible for my own life is easier than blaming others for whatever goes wrong.

____ Even if other people's decisions bother me at times, I know that they have to figure things out for themselves, and I don't give advice unless I am asked for it.

Competence:

____ I rely on learning and practice to succeed in life.

____ Competence is more about completing than competing.

____ I don't expect to be perfect right away, just good enough.

Dignity:

____ My sense of worth comes from inside me, not from who I hang out with.

____ When others gossip, I tell them I don't want to hear that stuff. I focus my life on things I consider really important.

____ I have an abiding sense of respect both for myself and others, so of course I am confident that we'll work things out for the best.

Humility:

____ I am no better and no worse than any other human being.

____ Each person is unique and important. I am glad I can share with others.

____ Who I am is more important than what I have, how I look, or how many other people I can beat in life.

Honor:

____ I can stand up for what I believe, even when others disagree.

____ I act out my real values in how I live.

____ Honesty and fair action help me believe in myself.

Purpose:

____ I believe that I have something important to contribute in life.

____ I have learned enough to catch myself when I get off track.

____ There is something important to me that I intend to do in life.

Vigor:

_____ I have found out how to have all the energy I really need to have.

_____ Being active in life is a good feeling.

_____ The older I get, the more alive and excited about life I feel.

Strength:

_____ I am a strong person.

_____ I use my strength to lead an exuberant life.

· _____ Being strong enough to let myself be human is hard, but it's getting easier the more I do it.

Integrity:

_____ Looking clearly at myself has helped me grow.

_____ To say one thing and do another weakens me from inside. I have learned to be more consistent.

_____ I have to be honest because I have learned that trusting myself is important.

Wholeness:

_____ A paradox is a contradiction where both sides are true. I am like that a lot more than I used to think I was.

_____ There are no "good" or "bad" feelings. It's all right to have the feelings I do have, as long as I behave appropriately.

_____ Variety is the spice of life, so I can appreciate differences in myself and in others.

Which of these opposites of shame have you most developed to help you through life? Which one would you most like to work on within the next year? What is one quality you could add to your life today that would make your life richer in a positive way? Answer these questions for yourself, and then practice that new attitude at every opportunity for the next week. At the end of the week, give yourself some praise for having tried it out, whether you mastered it or not.

Three Kinds of Shame, Three Pathways for Hope

Three Kinds of Shame

If there is one main message associated with shame, it's that "There is something essentially wrong with me." Shame always points out deficits, weaknesses, shortcomings. But can we be more specific about exactly what kind of weaknesses shame pinpoints? Or is shame always a blanket indictment, a general, global attack on someone's worthiness?

We have observed that people often describe three significant types of shame (there may be more types but these are the three that are most frequently mentioned). We have named them social shame, competence shame, and existential (being) shame. These three feel different to the person experiencing them, point out different problems, and lead toward hope along three slightly different pathways.

Understanding each can help you find the best way through, up, and out of the tangle of thoughts and emotions shame produces.

The first type of shame is called *social shame*. This shame drives people to fit in, to conform, to be acceptable. Social shame is the most easily identifiable shame because it is carefully woven into people's daily lives, affecting everything from the economic system to the social system.

It comes in two main varieties: group social shame and individual social shame. Although they overlap, there is one especially significant difference between them. Group social shaming is usually begun by outsiders, and is often called "prejudice" or "bias." We discussed group social shame in chapter 1.

Individual social shame may come from others or it may originate internally as the result of making comparisons. It centers around the question, "What will people think?" Social shame primarily develops around the fear of abandonment. "If I do something wrong, then I will be rejected. People will leave me. I will be all alone. I will not be allowed to belong." As noted in the preceding chapter, this fear of abandonment goes all the way back to the infant's need to be nurtured. Unable to survive on their own for years after birth, children naturally fear alienating the people who care for them. Social shame, then, acts to ensure that children, and later adults, don't say or do things that could lead to others' disapproval. Although social shame can become a weapon used by a group to "keep everyone in line," it's best use it to set general boundaries and standards for socially acceptable behavior that is for the greatest good of most people.

Competence shame comes next. The main belief here is, "I'm not good enough. I can't do anything right." Competence shame grows in the gap between what people can do and what they think they *should* do. When this kind of shame is at a toxic level, people with competence feel like frauds and failures. But competence shame also has value. It pushes people toward doing things well and toward accomplishing the tasks of which they can be most proud.

We call the third type of shame *existential shame*, or "being" shame. This is perhaps the most difficult of the three to work with because of its core message: "I am worthless. My life is meaningless. I have nothing to live for." Existential shame attacks a person's right to exist. This is the kind of shame that most often leaves people feeling hopeless about the meaning of their lives and that most predicts suicidality. On the other hand, existential shame can help people examine their activities more deeply. It often indicates the need for a profound change of purpose or overhaul of the basic circumstances in one's life and, used appropriately, leads to renewed action. People afflicted with shame about their being can interpret it as a call to search for something more they can do with their lives.

Our goal for the rest of this chapter is to look at the particular ways these three types of shame can affect people. We'll describe both the positive and negative aspects of social, competence, and existential shame. We'll also connect these three types of shame with three pathways of hope.

Social Shame

Social shame is about not belonging. Most everyone yearns to belong, to fit in, to have a place in the world. Alternatively, people dislike and sometimes come to dread being left alone, left out. Everyone learns to survive moments of aloneness, of course. People even discover the joys of solitude. It's sometimes nice to get away from others—to walk, read, think, write in privacy. Finding time to be alone with yourself can be tremendously rewarding. Indeed, solitude and privacy are wonderful—with one catch. That catch is about choice.

Aloneness is good and not scary as long as you are in charge of when and how much alone time you want; when it's your choice. But what if you need company, connection, union, belonging, and there's nobody there to join with? What if you feel as if the ropes that bond you to others have been cut, maybe forever? That's when people experience awful feelings of isolation. Utter loneliness can eat at a person's soul.

The "job" of social shame is to protect people from abandonment. Imagine, for a moment, that your social shame was standing outside of you, speaking to you, and that you were just a small child. Here's what your social shame might say: "Child, you need to learn a lesson about life. You've gotta fit in, Honey. You can't just go off being whoever you want to be, doing whatever you feel like doing. No, no, no. You try that and you'll be sorry. Mama won't smile at you. Daddy will be mean. Why, they might not even feed you if you're bad. So, Child, be nice. Do what they tell you, be what they want you to be. It's not so bad, you'll see."

You might imagine your social shame speaking to you with a really nice voice. Alternatively, you could be hearing a harsh, demanding "do it my way or else" voice. Either way, the idea is the same. Do and be what people want and you'll have a place. Failure to do and be what they want will get you punished.

When does social shame strike? At precisely the moment when people realize that something they've said or done is disapproved of by others. The eight-year-old daughter who thought she was pleasing her mother by baking some cookies only to be told she has no business in the kitchen by herself; the eighteen-year-old kid not allowed into her school's inner circle because she gets too many As; the twenty-eight-year old man who gets that nasty "You're making a fool of yourself again" look from his girlfriend while talking at a party; the thirty-eight-year-old woman whose best efforts to please her in-laws have once again been met with sighs of disinterest; the forty-eight-year-old whose wife of twenty years now says she finds him boring and wants a separation; the fifty-eight-year-old man whose best friends have been avoiding him since he told them he has cancer; the sixty-eight-year-old recent widow choosing to date again way too soon for her family; the seventy-eight-year-old couple encountering silent disapproval because they've decided to stay in their house instead of going to the nursing home their children selected.

Can't you hear the inner voice of shame reproaching these people: "You did it again, didn't you? Now _____ really dislikes you. Why don't you just forget about ever fitting in? You'll never belong. You're a loser." This voice often leads people to avoid social situations entirely. Convinced they are socially incompetent, they withdraw from human contact. Perhaps, though, someone's inner social critic isn't quite that mean. The message then sounds more like this: "You blew it. Now they're mad at you. But you can fit in. Just do what they say. Be what they want. Then they'll accept you." That voice leads people toward conformity, toward renouncing disapproved parts of themselves and overemphasizing acceptable characteristics.

A certain amount of social shame is positive and productive. After all, it is important to fit in. Perhaps nothing feels better than really feeling that you are accepted and appreciated. Moments of social shame help people recognize when they've done something that disrupts their smooth connections with others. Then they can choose to correct their behavior. You can repair the interpersonal bridge that links you with others before damage is too severe or extensive (Kaufman 1996). Most incidents of social shame do more good than harm, even though they feel awful when they happen.

Sometimes, unfortunately, social shame settles in for a long visit in a person's mind. It becomes what is called *characterological*—an apparently permanent part of someone's personality. People with this long-term social shame are convinced that they must hide their real selves from just about everybody. That's because they are convinced that if people got to know them they would certainly reject them. "Ugh ... yuck ... go away!" would be what others would think or say. "You're different. You don't belong. You're not one of us." In reality, others may or may not actually respond that way. What's important is that deeply socially shamed persons expect rejection of their real selves.

People with this extreme level of belonging shame dread exposure of their real, supposedly bad selves. Consequently, they may go to great lengths to conceal their basic natures. Some become social chameleons, changing by the moment, hour, day, and situation as they try to please people. Others develop what are called false selves. They do so by rejecting completely those parts of themselves that others dislike. If a father can't tolerate passivity in his son, then the son may have to give up everything but his "doer" qualities, becoming a nonstop, nonfeeling workaholic in the process. That boy's urges to be more passive and less controlling of the world may be shoved deep into his unconscious. Since he can't be both passive and loved by his dad he becomes totally active.

The fear of rejection has much to do with our fast-paced society's stress on appearance and image. "How do I look?" becomes an especially critical question when people don't really get to know each other very well. Indeed, many individuals and families seem to be more concerned with appearance than reality. As long as they look good, as long as they can maintain appearances, then everything must be okay. Shame has come to dominate these people. Or, more correctly, it's their fear of shameful rejection that controls them.

When is social shame most likely to appear? The general answer is whenever one's public identity is threatened or when one's private identity is exposed. People's public identities consist mostly of the roles they play (parent, teacher, and so on), the style with which they enact those roles (the particular way they parent, teach, and so on), the kind of person they want others to think they are (kind, competitive, wise . . .), and a clear idea of whom they are not (a country boy, a risk taker, a star, a loner . . .). That public identity isn't the sum of a person, though. People also have private identities more or less compatible with what they let others see. Most people's private identities harbor a few secrets that they wouldn't want others to know about, ways that they act when they let down our hair, and even their ability to share the most intimate and personal parts of their feelings, experiences, and desires.

Public identities are a little like masks that people wear whenever they're in view. But, unlike a mask, which you might casually throw away when used, people take their public personas very seriously. Your public persona is a part of you, just as real as the private identity partially hidden by the public one. So it's definitely painful when someone says something that challenges our public identity. Imagine, for example, the reaction of a priest accused of sexually molesting a member of the church or the humiliation that comes with being suddenly fired from your job and escorted out of the workplace by uniformed security persons. At a considerably lesser level (because it doesn't challenge core identity features), imagine someone's embarrassment when told they have a spot on their suit or a rip in their pants.

With rare exceptions, consistency is one of the key aspects of public identity. People are expected to be pretty much the same day after day. That's why they attempt to repair any damage to their public images as quickly as possible. They want to clear their good names, you might say, so that people once again think of them in the "right" way.

Any sudden or uncontrolled exposure of one's private self almost certainly will be accompanied by shame. The son whose mother whips out his baby pictures to show his new girlfriend; the congressman who is "outed" as a homosexual by a militant gay rights organization; the grief-stricken parents whose tears are videotaped for the local television news just as they learn their child has drowned. Something very personal and private has been exposed with each of these persons. They might very well feel both embarrassed and violated by the unexpected attention. Needless to add, their sense of shame will be much worsened if their private selves are judged by others to be a bad.

Let's summarize what we've said so far about social shame. First, it's based on the fear of abandonment. Second, moments of social shame tell people that they are in danger of disconnection—that they've done or said something that could get them rejected. Third, this information allows people to make a choice: quit doing what's unacceptable and start doing what others want or risk isolation. Fourth, that social shame is triggered under two conditions, either when your public image is threatened or when your private self is suddenly exposed.

Now that you have a good understanding of what social shame is, where it comes from, and what it tells you, you're in a good position to begin to transform it into a positive force in your life. The next section will begin to explain how.

Social Pride: The First Pathway of Hope

We've written in chapter 2 how the word "pride" summarizes the journey out of excessive shame. Social pride, then, comes about when people feel good about their social selves. The signs of this positive feeling are that people feel comfortable with others, sense that they do belong, and that they're capable of bonding and intimacy. All in all, these people believe that they have a place in the universe so they do not excessively fear rejection and abandonment.

There are five main things you can do to improve your sense of social pride:

- recognize and deal with the effects of past abandonments and rejections;

- address how your fear of abandonment has affected and continues to affect your life;

- rediscover and accept hidden parts of yourself that have been discarded because of social shame;

- develop a network of nonshaming, nonblaming friends and associates;

- develop a sense of belonging at all levels of your being, including spiritually.

Deal with Past Rejections

Where does the fear of abandonment come from? Aside from the instinctual childhood fear we've spoken of, this fear frequently emerges as an aftereffect of actual losses and rejections. In other words, the fear of abandonment reflects the fact of abandonment in your life history. It's important to recognize what's happened to you without either minimizing or exaggerating your wounds. One way to begin is for you to make a list (in your journal, if you've been keeping one, or in a separate notebook) of the major times, both as a child and adult, that you've been abandoned or rejected. You'll want to focus upon those episodes that burned into your soul the most, even if they might seem small to others—things like always getting picked last on schoolyard sports teams because you were clumsy or having to wear out-of-fashion clothes in high school because your parents had less money than other kids' parents.

Address Your Fear of Abandonment

All the past rejections in the world would be insignificant if they could be left behind. But what if they've snuck into the present? What if they haunt you in the form of a fear of doing anything that might get you rejected once again? Or perhaps you've become convinced that you'll certainly be rejected no matter what you do, so why bother even trying to get close to others?

That's why the second step on the road to social pride is discovering how your fear of abandonment affects your current life. What do you do because of your need to fit in? What don't you do? How much of your life revolves around the fear of rejection? Also, how realistic are your fears? It's one thing if, in fact, you live or work with hostile, perpetually rejecting shamers. It's quite different, though, if you expect people to be more rejecting than they really are. That happens when people have an irrational fear of abandonment.

Hidden Discoveries

We've written about how people sometimes abandon certain parts of themselves so as not to be rejected. Part of the process of healing excessive social shame is to discover and reclaim those missing aspects of yourself. Thus, someone who jettisoned their intensity to please an unemotional parent might reclaim the right to passion; someone who gave up the right to play might join an adult hobby group; a person who disowned creativity may take up poetry. To do so will almost certainly be scary at first. It will trigger feelings of shame and fear of abandonment. Eventually, though, healing occurs when people rediscover all that they are.

New Friends

One of the best ways to heal social shame is to spend as much time as possible with nonshaming people. What could be better than knowing that your friends and family want you in their lives? They don't just tolerate you. They don't sneer at you. No, they really do appreciate you and look forward to your company. It's true that you have to accept and acknowledge their interest and caring. That's your job. But it's sure a lot easier to do that when people genuinely like you. So find people who open a place for you in the circle of love—and then step into that circle with joy.

A Sense of Belonging

The final healing of excessive social shame happens when people truly sense they have a place in the universe. This means far more than merely fitting in. It means believing that your life has value, your contribution is significant, and your existence matters to others. It requires a sense of belonging on a wider, more spiritual level. You become part of the goodness in the universe, part of the whole. You are more able to accept others as well, since they, too, are connected to one shared universe. This larger sense of belonging leads beyond connection to communion, the feeling of being emotionally united and committed to others as complete people part of a larger whole. The fear of abandonment subsides when, feeling whole and complete, someone feels safely at one with the world.

Competence Shame

There are five core shame messages: "I am not good; I'm not good enough; I don't belong; I'm unlovable; I should not be." Of these, "I'm not good enough," is the one cited most commonly by the bulk of American clients and students we've met. It's unclear if this is cultural or universal, but certainly the American emphasis upon competitive and comparative performance contributes greatly to people's sense of never quite being competent. "Succeed, succeed, succeed!" our society preaches. "Be number one. Don't settle for less. Be ambitious. Strive. You can be anything you want to be. You can do anything you want to do. Shame on you if you aren't the best. If you're not perfect, you're a failure." This country's work ethic is obviously a two-edged sword. The very forces that push you toward working hard and driving toward accomplishment prevent you from knowing when to stop pushing. Merciless competition breeds a fear of failure. And this fear of failure promotes competence shame, that sense of never being good enough.

Competence shame is likely to pop up whenever you makes a mistake. In those situations it's all too easy to go from "I made a mistake" to "I am a mistake," from "I failed that one time" to "I am a total failure." People with competence shame feel weak, inadequate, and ineffective. Every error they make simply verifies, to them, their intrinsic defectiveness. No wonder so many people become perfectionists, always trying to stay one step ahead of their shame. But perfectionism only delays competence shame. It doesn't alleviate or heal it. Because human beings are all flawed, they inevitably slip up. The perfectionist flounders for a moment, just long enough to hear the inner condemnation: "You're lousy. You're a fraud. You're can't do anything right. You're a loser."

Competence shame arises on other occasions as well. Falling short of your goals and ideals might trigger shame, such as when the loaves of bread you've prepared so painstakingly come out of the oven burned, or realizing at age sixty that you've "peaked" and will never become president of the firm. Another major source of competence shame happens when people can't stop comparing themselves with others. Then the question isn't, "Am I good enough," but, "Am I better than ____." Just asking that kind of comparative query paves the road for shame. You may be better than someone else today, but initiating that sort of competing means that you have to worry about all the possible defeats that could take place with others tomorrow.

Competence shame does have one redeeming value: it reminds people to feel bad when they don't work honestly at their task. That is it's main purpose. Without competence shame people certainly would have little to take pride in. The problem, as we have said with all kinds of shame, occurs when people feel too much competence shame. Then, instead of prodding people to do as well as they can, this shame becomes debilitating. Feeling like a perpetual failure, never adequate, only leads to withdrawal from challenges and hindrances to your success.

The flip side of competence shame is competence pride. The steps that help move people toward competence pride are these:

- make a commitment to utilize your strengths and compensate for your weaknesses;
- learn to accept the idea of being good enough rather than perfect;
- set reasonable targets and goals for yourself;
- move toward psychologically challenging tasks;
- compare yourself only with yourself.

Strengths and Weaknesses

Each human being has natural gifts. One person may be great with numbers, be impressively athletic, and have a good facility with words. Another is gentle, artistic, and tactile. On the other hand, everyone also has their weaknesses. The numbers person may lack organizational skills, the tactile artist may not intuitively grasp perspective.

Shame and pride don't exactly reflect our natural strengths and deficits. After all, what pride can someone take, for instance, in having an IQ of 150? Lucky, yes, to be born that smart. But competence shame and pride must be *earned*. It's how you use your natural gifts that determines whether you'll feel good about yourself. People feel competence pride when they do something as well as they reasonably can. There are two ways to get that pride. First, you can use your natural gifts well; second, you can compensate appropriately for your weaknesses. The natural athlete gets help in devising an organizational system to use. The tactile artist takes classes on perspective to minimize that deficit or possibly concentrates on creating scenes that lessen the need for perspective.

What are your natural gifts? Your natural deficits? It's really important to be honest with yourself as you make up this mental list. Overestimating your gifts ("Hey, I'm great at everything. I'm a natural genius") only leads to disappointment when the rest of the world fails to worship your brilliance. Underestimating ("I'm awful at everything. I'm a complete failure") locks in your shame and keeps you from accomplishing anything.

Good Enough

The next step in developing competence pride is learning to live by the principle of "good enough." This is particularly crucial if you're a perfectionist or if you stop yourself from doing things because you might not do them right.

When is something you do good enough? Usually, when you run into the law of diminishing returns, meaning that you've begun putting more energy into a project than you're getting value out of it. Here's an example. Say you want to learn how to plant a garden, something you've never done or observed. So, you read a book and learn a lot. Inspired, you read another book, and another. But sooner or later you realize that you already know almost everything in them. You've reached the good enough point where you can go outside and successfully plant that garden. Certainly you could keep reading and reading, but it won't give your gardening project any more benefit.

Reasonable Goals

There's often a gap between what we've done so far with our lives and what we want to accomplish. That's because each person has an "ideal self" in mind. Your ideal self is you at your finest. The gap between real and ideal can actually be very productive. It can pull you toward developing your skills. But sometimes the gap seems too wide, an unbridgable chasm that makes you only too aware of your inadequacies. You feel competence shame when you don't see any way to move toward your goals. By contrast, people experience competence pride by moving toward their ideals, even if they never completely reach them. Setting reasonable, achievable goals is one important way to honor your ideal self and feel competence pride.

Reasonable goals usually focus upon process instead of product. For example, the writer who commits to writing three pages a day is more likely to succeed than the one who simply decides to write when inspired. Both want to write, all right. But one has a plan while the other only a wish.

Accept Challenges

Competence pride rises when people accept a few challenges in their lives. What will they do next? What risks will they take? People with competence pride seek new areas to develop their talents. They're willing to risk occasional failure in order to acquire new skills. So, when they have an opportunity to branch out, they usually accept the invitation.

Efficacy researchers note that effective doers have what they call a "coping response" (Bandura 1997). When pressed, they move toward challenge rather than run away from it. Accepting challenges like that increases your self-worth. It helps you believe you can cope with a constantly changing world. One way, then, to increase self-esteem and competence pride is to ask yourself what challenges that have come your way lately you're going to accept.

Don't Compare with Others

Competence pride is an intensely personal commodity. It involves feeling good about what you do based on your own skills and abilities. That's why most competitive runners compete against themselves even more than with the other runners in a race. Their goal is to better their own performance more than to beat everybody else. Instead of comparing themselves with others they compare their current times with their own past times.

Shame thrives when people spend too much time comparing themselves with others. Excessive comparison also promotes envy, the wish for others to lose whatever has brought them joy. But others' defeats doesn't lead to real pride for you. The only path to competence pride is committing to do something well and keeping that promise to yourself.

Existential (Being) Shame

Have you ever found yourself doubting your right to exist? Thinking that you were worthless, a burden, maybe even God's mistake? Convinced that the world would be far better off if you weren't in it? Feeling empty, cut off not so much from others, but from your own self? Believing that the answer to the question, "Who am I?" is, "Nobody—nothing"? Not necessarily suicidal, but feeling that your life was hopeless and meaningless? All these are signs of existential shame.

Existential shame happens when the self abandons the self. But how and why does this occur? From a family-of-origin perspective, the answer is that children sense they are unwanted by their parents. Instead of feeling the warm glow of love in their parents' eyes, they see only indifference and annoyance. They soon decide that there must be something basically, fundamentally wrong with them. They decide that it can't be their parents' fault or inadequacy that makes them unable to bond with their children. After all, it would be too threatening to think that the people solely responsible for one's survival are so fatally flawed. It must be the child's own fault. Something is intrinsically wrong with them. They are fatally flawed. They begin to turn away from themselves with contempt and disgust. They disown their right to exist.

This is certainly a compelling explanation, but we need to urge caution. There are alternative explanations that exempt your family of origin from responsibility. It's possible that you're suffering from a long-term biochemically caused depression. Certainly, anyone who experiences these thoughts and feelings should get an assessment for depression from a mental health professional. It's also important to consider other sources of shame such as your current relationships and cultural prejudices. Lastly, remember that ultimately, as an adult you must take responsibility for your own life. If you are renouncing your own existence, then only *you* can reclaim the right to be.

There's one more possible explanation for existential shame. It could be that just about everybody has moments of shame like this, times when they question the core meaning of their lives. After all, you're not born with a little fortune-cookie slip telling you why you're here. You must search out the deeper purpose of your existence and deal with despair at those times when your purpose seems illusive.

Like all shame, existential shame is valuable when it is short-term, not too intense, and when it gives you a message, such as, "Well, do you really want to work at Billy's Bagels the rest of your life? What happened to your promise to help others as well as yourself?" Existential shame like this that leads to the possibility of existential pride is useful. That's very different from being buried in layers of toxic existential shame in which you can't imagine ever accepting yourself or discovering meaning in your life.

There are four ways you can move from existential shame to existential pride. They are:

- confront your self-destroyer;
- become curious about yourself;
- search for what does give meaning to your life;
- affirm your right to be.

Confront Your Self-Destroyer

This advice is critically important for those with excessive amounts of existential shame. If that's you, think of your existential shame as if it were a schoolyard bully. It yells, intimidates, threatens to annihilate you. The more you give in to it, the weaker you feel. That bully thrives on your fear and shame.

There's only one way to deal with a bully. Stand up and fight. When that bully says you're worthless, insist that's a lie. True, you might get beaten up a few times, but that doesn't really matter. You've got to keep fighting until your bully finally understands that you won't go along with condemning yourself any longer. You may never dislodge that bully completely from your mind, but at least you can limit its power and control over you.

Become Curious

Existentially shamed people often have lost interest in themselves. They don't know who they are and they don't care. Why should they when they believe that they are basically defective? Who wants to find out more and more about their flaws?

It's important to rekindle interest in the self to heal existential shame. That means wondering about who you are, where you're going, and what makes you tick. Of course, you need to notice the good stuff in you, not just the bad, so that you can see yourself as fully human. Becoming curious like this is a major component of self-acceptance. You cannot accept yourself until you know who you are.

Search for Meaning

Meaningful lives don't just happen. They result from people thoughtfully considering what they need to do and how they want to be. Perhaps no single activity or career is always meaningful. One priest may find perfect value in his life while another secretly feels he's wasting his time. One nurse longs to quit her boring job while her colleague can't wait for another day's work. Nor are cultural judgments invariably useful. Just because American society rewards bankers more than social workers doesn't necessarily mean that bankers will feel better about their lives.

So, it becomes your personal responsibility to seek out meaning in your life. What can you do that fills you with pride? What would you like to be remembered for after you die? What would you most regret failing to do in your life? On a day-to-day basis, what activities feel valuable? How are you contributing to the world in ways that help you feel good about yourself?

Don't get caught up in the search for the one perfect job, contribution, or activity. Chances are, there are many things that could add significantly to your sense of personal worth. Certainly, every day each person contributes to the common good in some way or another. The goal here is to discover which of many possible socially meaningful endeavors feels right to you.

Affirm Your Being

Doesn't it seem strange that anyone would have to affirm their basic right to exist? It's not as if you asked to be created or that you signed a promissory contract upon birth. Wouldn't it make sense instead to believe that there is value to your life simply because you're here?

"I am." "I exist." These are simple but critical statements in healing existential shame. Notice that they are nonjudgmental. Existential pride is simply an affirmation that you exist, not that you are good or bad. The ultimate healing of existential shame occurs when you can affirm the meaningfulness of your very being. You have value on this planet regardless of what you do. Your very being is a unique work of art that can never be duplicated.

Another way of describing this is to say that you yourself are the meaning of your existence. Yes, certainly, you want to contribute your share to the world, and you will. But your very existence is intrinsically worthwhile. That's why you need never question your right to exist. You are—and that's enough.

Exercises

1. A chameleon is a lizard whose skin changes color to match its environment. If it is sitting in the sand, its skin turns brown; if it is on a dark gray rock, its skin turns dark gray. This provides good camouflage so that others can't see it very well, if at all. Many shame-based individuals are like the chameleon, changing themselves to try to fit invisibly into whatever environment they're in. Afraid to stand out too much, they become like whoever they happen to be around at the time. The problem arises when they do this too often, and even they lose track of exactly who they are. Think about some times when you changed your behavior to fit in with the people around you, so they wouldn't perceive you as "different." How did you think they would judge you and what did you think they might do then? What did you gain by hiding? What did you lose by hiding?

2. Often, the best antidote for rejection is to explore it instead of just fear it. The goal of this exercise is to get twenty *real* rejections. Now, if you call someone up and ask them to do something with you when they have something else already planned, that is not a real rejection. If you call and say, "I know you won't want to do this with me," and they say "No, I don't," that's not a real rejection, either. A real rejection is a "No, I don't want to do that with you" that is not a set-up and not a rejection you have actually asked for. Asking a person who never does anything with anybody doesn't count, either.

    But, if you would like to overcome your fear of rejection, set out to get twenty *real* rejections. You might think the goal is just to get used to being rejected. But there is a catch to this exercise, a utility to actually calling up enough people to get those twenty rejections. You may find that, after you have called just a few, you will be very busy doing things as a result of the acceptances you have gotten. Other folks who have tried this have discovered that their datebooks quickly filled up. The acceptances, in every case, more than balanced out the rejections when people figured out how to ask for what they really wanted. So, try challenging yourself to get twenty real rejections and keep track of your results. When you get an acceptance and suddenly get scared, remember that anxiety is just inside-out excitement, and go explore that acceptance anyway.

3. Many shamed individuals have trouble accepting praise from others because they are so critical of themselves. When someone compliments them, they think that person is either being "nice" (phony) or has poor judgment, because inside the shamed person is sure that there is something wrong with them. Do you have trouble accepting praise from others? What do you say in your head when you get a compliment—or do you reverse the compliment so quickly you don't even hear it? What do you say out loud: do you accept, reject, or discount the compliment or the person giving it? For the next several days practice breathing in when you get a compliment. Take a big, deep breath and let the compliment penetrate. Then exhale again before you respond. Do the same for hugs, pats, smiles, and thank-you's. This is an easy and surprisingly helpful way to take care of yourself.

4. "Practice makes perfect," goes the adage, and it's a good one. The more you do things, the better you'll get at them, generally—unless you're really not suited for them or unless you are too anxious and worried about being perfect to keep doing them. That happens when you tell yourself untrue things like, "Because I didn't get it right this time, I'll never get it right." It happens to children, too, if you cut off their learning with an angry, "Can't you do anything right?" or an overprotective, "Let me do it for you. You'll spill it."

    Here are some exercises to help you explore your competence shame until you fully understand it.

    a) If you are a perfectionist about clothes, wear your solid-colored blazer for an entire day, and no matter what, *don't pick off any lint*. Examine your feelings as you go through the day; use a journal to record your experience; and remember that if others notice, they'll probably just feel a bit more relaxed around you.

    b) This week, make one intentional error each day. Misspell an important word at the office, burn the rice, wear unmatched socks, sing the wrong words to a song, get someone the wrong thing before you get the right one, put the fitted sheet on top. If none of your errors are noticed, try a few more until they are. When your mistakes are noticed, remember that you are still in control, since you made that mistake on purpose. Or, the next time you make a mistake, try pretending you did it on purpose. Write the words "lighten up" on the inside of your hand and look at it frequently.

c) Identify an area you might like, but have given up learning because you feel you're not very good at it. Then go ahead and take a class in that area. Whenever you start to measure your progress by comparing yourself to others, *stop*. Keep track of your progress only in comparison to where you were when you began to learn again.

d) A mantra is a saying that you repeat over and over to yourself, until you fully understand and can be in accordance with it. Choose one of the following statements for a mantra and say it to yourself several times a day.

"Good enough is good enough."

"I am perfectly human."

"Don't let yesterday use up today."

"Everything has a beginning."

"I am."

"I belong."

"I am competent."

5. Existential shame heals as you learn who you are and what your purpose in life might be. We figure that each person here on earth has something to learn and something to give. If you are still here on this earth, then, obviously, your "homework" is not finished. There is something left to learn and to do in the world before you will have finished. Perhaps learning how to value yourself more is a necessary step to finding out what your job here is. Answer each of the following questions ten times on paper. If you can't get ten different answers now, concentrate on finding out what they might be and add them later. If you get ten answers but you don't see some of them as positive, choose one of those answers at a time to change into ones you would like to have in your life.

   · Question 1: "Who Am I?"
   · Question 2: "Who Am I Becoming?"

Your Hidden Yearnings: The Secret Message of Shame

What Are Yearnings?

Charlie Mayes has been driving a truck for twenty years now. He's getting old for such heavily physical work, and his body is beginning to break down. A recovering alcoholic, he's going through what people in Alcoholics Anonymous sometimes call a "dry drunk," or a period of sobriety when the person still feels rotten. Charlie's irritable at home, bored at work, vaguely anxious, a little depressed. When asked what he yearns for, Charlie first says, "I don't know," and changes the subject. When asked again, he gets a far away, wistful look in his eyes. "I just want to be happy again," he says, and begins to cry. Charlie had never been happy in childhood, himself growing up with alcoholic and abusive parents. In fact, he used to sneer at anyone who thought happiness was important, telling them to grow up. But then, for a little while after he sobered up, he felt happy. Really, honestly content. Now Charlie desperately wants this new friend back. He yearns for happiness.

Annette Thomas tells herself she should be satisfied. After all, she's got a good job as a furniture designer in New York City, two well-behaved and loving children, and a decent marriage. And yet she yearns for something more. "I feel so shallow," she remarks. She'd like to pursue something more spiritual, some job or activity that would feel more meaningful. But just then Annette feels embarrassed, as if somehow she shouldn't think or say that. She's had this feeling before but never paid much attention to it. Now she realizes that she's feeling shame. "Isn't that odd?" she thinks. "I feel shame every time I start thinking about searching for a deeper purpose in life. I wonder why?"

Annette's question is a good one, and you may have also experienced feelings of shame when thinking about things that you truly wanted. This is because sometimes shame is used to make people give up their deepest wants, needs, wishes, and dreams. The parent who says, "Now, now, it's nice that you want to be a doctor but we need you to get a business degree and come back to run the farm," or the spouse who says, "No, don't quit you job to take care of the kids. That's stupid!" generate feelings of shame in the person for listening to their real desires. But before we explain this connection, we'll explain a little bit more what we mean by "yearnings."

We are mental-health therapists; and, in our experience, most people come to counseling with specific problems: their marriages are falling apart, they feel anxious or depressed, they can't decide what they want to do with their lives, they have problems controlling their tempers. But no matter what the initial problem, they've all had a powerful response to one simple question: "What do you yearn for?" That question makes people pause. They get a distant look in their eyes, a wistful, dreamy gaze. Then they begin to talk, often about long-forgotten wishes and wants.

"I yearn for wisdom."

"I yearn to be creative."

"I yearn for ecstasy."

"I yearn to feel loved."

"I yearn for peace."

"I yearn to wander and discover."

"I yearn for wealth."

"I yearn for control."

"I yearn to feel safe."

"I yearn to find God."

"I yearn for knowledge."

"I yearn . . ." "I yearn . . ." "I yearn."

What are yearnings? A dictionary definition of a yearning is, "a deep longing, especially when accompanied by tenderness or sadness." (*Random House Unabridged Dictionary*, Second Edition, 1993).

Yearnings are special. They are more than thoughts or feelings. They are intensely private and personal declarations of what could provide each person with their greatest security, satisfaction, and joy. Yearnings are delicate and fragile, easily shamed into the background of awareness. It only takes a few "Oh, now you're being stupid, you shouldn't want that" messages for yearnings to retreat and go into hiding. But yearnings are also amazingly durable. They may hide, but they never go away completely. Yearnings are always ready to be retrieved, awaiting only a good time to emerge and reannounce themselves. Like seeds in the desert, they can endure years of drought and then flower beautifully when finally nurtured. The only difference is that yearnings are nurtured not with water but with a safe environment, curiosity, encouragement, and healthy pride.

Yearnings come from within. They are rooted within the unconscious part of the brain, which means that they aren't always consciously known. A yearning is part thought, part feeling. It usually carries with it a "Yes, that's exactly what I want to do with my life" sense of certainty, if and when you become aware of it. A yearning can often be envisioned in an idyllic scene: picture yourself being wherever you most want to be, doing whatever you most want to do, with whomever you most want to be near. That combination of place, activity, and connection may very well represent your yearnings as they are played out in your unconscious mind, especially if you feel safe, comforted, peaceful, content, and, at the same time, a little exhilarated by your image.

Yearnings don't make sense. They aren't logical, realistic, or commonsensical. On the other hand, they aren't illogical, unrealistic, or senseless, either. They are nonrational, deeply compelling inner voices. The lead character in the movie *Field of Dreams*, driven to build a ballpark in the middle of an Iowa corn field, is responding to a yearning, although with far more drama than in real life. While his motto was, "Build it, and they will come," a more accurate statement about yearnings would be, "Build it, and you will feel deeply satisfied whether or not anyone comes."

Yearnings are like melodies privately composed for only one person. But, although each song is unique, it's possible to describe the notes that go into each tune. The song of yearning is composed of the following notes:

One's deepest desires. The single most insistent beat in the song of our yearnings is this: yearnings, when you listen to them, tell you about your deepest desires. Yearnings carry with them a feeling of rightness. People sense the word "Yes" when they discover their yearnings. "Yes, this is me. Yes, this is right."

Each human being has a wide range of possible lives that honor their yearnings. A woman who would go to college and become a high school French and German teacher might use some of the same skills to become a tour guide to remote regions of the world or a computer software designer who speaks fluently in that mysterious language. Perhaps, though, fate has taken her entirely away from a career in language. Still, she yearns to discover and literally to think differently about things (which is one of the most important aspects of being multilingual). To fulfill her deep desire, perhaps she could, for example, travel widely throughout the world on holidays or volunteer to teach English as a foreign language?

Compelling. Yearnings feel compelling. That's why they are stronger than mere "wants." A want feels good when met and frustrating when unmet. But a yearning is stronger than that. A yearning feels wonderful when met and terribly disappointing when not. Imagine, for instance, how the woman above would feel if her long-planned trip to Turkey were suddenly canceled. While her spouse might be annoyed, she could feel devastated. Her husband only wanted to travel abroad. She yearned to hear another language actually being spoken, to mingle in the crowds of a foreign city, to walk long-unknown roads just listening to all the unfamiliar sounds, to begin thinking from an entirely different perspective.

Longing for what seems unobtainable. A soldier, stationed thousands of miles from home, longs for the sights and sounds of his native land. A couple, having spent years trying to conceive, hope against hope one day to raise a family. A seriously injured athlete swears she'll play again at the top of her form, even while her friends doubt she'll ever be able to walk normally. Each of these people yearns for something almost but perhaps not quite unobtainable.

Yearnings are the stuff of dreams but also of heartbreak. Perhaps that's why people are so often discouraged from yearning by those who would protect them from pain. "Oh, honey, don't think of becoming a _____. The competition's too tough. You'll be happier with an ordinary career, anyhow." The message is, don't dream; don't yearn; don't ask yourself what would bring you the most satisfaction in life. Still, people continue to dream. Their yearnings refuse to die, even though they may be pushed far into the background by immediate necessity.

Private and personal. Yearnings are essentially private communications, messages from the psychological interior of your being. They often can best be accessed through journaling, quiet walks, and other kinds of introspection. Yearnings can be communicated to others, but they can never be completely shared. In other words, one person can tell another that they yearn, what they yearn for, and how that yearning feels to them. However, the listener, no matter how interested, can never hope fully to understand or to feel the other's specific yearning. This is true even if both happen to yearn for the same thing.

This limiting factor can be subtle and frustrating. Consider a couple named Pat and Jan who are trying to figure out why they've been arguing. Their troubles began after they sold their home in the city and bought a modest ranch. Jan and Pat thought their motivations for the move were identical. But they were actually just different enough to cause problems. Pat envisioned hard work, horses and cattle, wind and rain, fence mending, proud weather-beaten faces, tired bodies. Pat yearned to do battle with the elements. Meanwhile, Jan dreamt about growing herbs, sitting reading by a fire, laughing with friends, horse-drawn buggies, country dancing. Jan yearned for simplicity. So, when the idea of buying the ranch came up they both jumped at it because that ranch fit into their separate yearnings. Unfortunately, they neglected to inquire about the deepest reasons each wanted that property. They both mistakenly thought they completely understood the other. Now Pat nags Jan to work faster and harder while Jan complains that Pat keeps them so busy they can't enjoy the beauty that surrounds them.

Intuitive. Imagine a woman sorting through dozens of necklaces at a store or sale, just letting them sift through her hands while apparently gazing absent-mindedly at them. That woman's thoughts might sound like this: "No, no, pretty but not quite, no, not for me, no, no, ugh, here's one for my friend, no, no, no—ahh! That's the one." She's discovered the perfect necklace for her, the one that feels absolutely correct. Chances are excellent, too, others will agree when she shows them the necklace that it is indeed exactly suited for her. They will praise her intuition.

People discover their yearnings in a similar way. Each person goes through an internal sorting process, sifting through their possible life goals. Knowledge, experience, and education all help people sort through their possibilities, but the final selection process emerges from deep within. One or two possibilities eventually stand out as the things they could do with their lives that would bring them the greatest satisfaction.

Bittersweet. Yearnings are bittersweet. They seldom bring someone undivided pleasure. Rather, they fill the individual with feelings of tenderness, wistfulness, and sadness. That's because yearnings both connect you with your deepest desires and make you aware of the distance between where you are now and where you want to go with your life. To sense your yearnings means both to know what is most important to you personally and to recognize that you might never fully realize your destiny.

Action oriented. Yearnings are action oriented. They impel people to do something meaningful with their lives. Acting on your yearnings may be the world's best antidepressant: "I used to be so depressed, but now I'm doing what I want. Now when I wake up in the morning I'm glad to be alive."

There is a special quality to action taken in the service of a yearning. That action often feels natural, instinctive, amazingly easy—even if it seems as though it ought to be difficult. Your body and mind feel gracefully connected. Yearnings require action for completion. Action changes yearnings from dreams into reality.

Persistent. Like the hero in Gabriel Garcia Marquez' *Love in the Time of Cholera* (1988), who secretly loves a woman for decades before finally winning her, yearnings endure for a lifetime. They persist even when ignored for long periods. Indeed, they never disappear completely although they may be reduced to hanging around at the edges of awareness.

Yearnings act differently than wants or drives. They aren't as immediately compelling as drives, which demand that you eat, sleep, eliminate, or climax *now*. Nor do they have the "this would be nice, really great" luxury feel of a want. Rather, the power of yearnings is in their tenacity. They simply won't go away.

Imagine that someone takes a battery operated radio down to a brook. Then they turn the radio on full blast and sit down next to it. Needless to say, that person cannot hear the brook's murmurings. But eventually, perhaps hours or days later, the battery will start wearing down. Then the brook's gentle sounds can be heard. It's at this point that the listener has to make a choice—to head back to the house for more batteries or to listen to the brook. But, whatever the choice, the brook will keep flowing. It will be there the next time that person comes around, and the next. Indeed, the "brooks" of your yearnings never dry up. They run the entire length of your life.

Elusive. Yearnings are difficult to observe clearly. Indeed, they seem to operate in the waking space between dreams and reality, more sensed than seen. This elusive quality only adds to their allure. Yearnings are mysterious and wonderful, much like the northern lights that occasionally envelope the sky in their fragile dance. But why are yearnings so elusive? As persistent as they can be, why can they simultaneously seem so fragile and delicate?

The answer is that yearnings are intensely private. They reveal the deepest, most vulnerable aspects of ourselves both to you and to others. This part of the self is easily shamed into hiding. And, once shamed, people become extremely cautious about letting anyone, sometimes even their own selves, notice them. Eventually your yearnings act like stealthy deer at the edge of a woods ready to plunge back into shelter at the slightest sign of danger.

Meaningful/Spiritual. Yearnings help people discover what they must do with their lives in order to feel that they've made a meaningful contribution to the universe. Because of that, yearnings have spiritual significance. Indeed, attending to your yearnings helps you discover the linkages between the intimate nature of your being and the infinite nature of the universe. Honoring your yearnings means asking yourself some very important questions, each of which has profound spiritual implications: What gives your life meaning? How can you be true to yourself? How can you contribute to the greater good? What do you really want to do with your life before you die? Which of your daily activities are filled with spirit? Yearnings, then, connect people with that which is most important personally while helping them discover their connections with the whole.

Internal guides. We can summarize what we've written so far by saying that *yearnings are internal guides that help you discover your deepest wants, needs, and desires.* They often come to us during moments of quiet or contemplation, rewarding your efforts to learn more about who you are, where you belong, what you could do, and how to find meaning in your life. Yearnings bridge the gap between the conscious and unconscious parts of your mind, between the figurative and the literal, between the mundane and the spiritual.

People can survive without ever thinking about their yearnings or trying to find or follow them. But life becomes richer and far more full of beauty and meaning when your yearnings are honored.

Shame: The Marker for Yearnings

Now that you have a deeper understanding of the importance of yearnings in your life, we can begin to describe in more detail the role shame plays in the fulfillment of your yearnings. We've mentioned earlier in this chapter that shame can drive yearnings into hiding. Certainly it doesn't take too many "You're an idiot to want . . ." to make most people renounce their dreams. Telling others who are hostile or indifferent about your yearnings is like trying to grow a garden in a goat pasture. Those goats won't just eat the plants as they struggle out of the ground. They'll tear up the very soil they're planted in. Sadly, this world is all too full of human goats, those people always ready both to chew up another's most cherished hopes and to attack the person for even daring to dream.

If that were all, though, yearnings would hide from others but be easy for their owners to detect. But often that's not the case at all. Instead, it seems that many people have great difficulty discovering their own yearnings. That's because shame can so easily become internalized. What started out as somebody else shaming you turns into you shaming yourself. Then you become the goat in your own garden, tearing out the seedlings of your dreams. No wonder your yearnings become elusive, lurking on the fringes of consciousness until they sense they will be nurtured rather than attacked. Only then, when you learn to respect your yearnings, will those yearnings stand still long enough for you to see what they really look like.

Shame drives people away from their yearnings. The internal message in shame fits the formula "I want it, but . . ." (Kaufman 1996). While normal shame completes this message by saying, "I want it, but I may have to wait until later to get it," excessive shame alters the message to, "I want it, but I don't deserve it, shouldn't want it, and I'll never get it." The more shame affects someone the more their yearnings become like pebbles thrown into the waters of their minds, sinking without a trace into the recesses of the unconscious.

Fortunately, though, people seldom succeed in completely burying their yearnings. Traces remain, often showing up in subtle signs such as momentary slips of the tongue or hesitations as you talk, unexpected blushes, or a sudden difficulty in making eye contact. These "don't go there" messages from within announce that the fear of feeling shame is blocking your self-awareness as well as your willingness to discuss openly some concern or desire.

Paradoxically, then, shame serves as a marker for hidden yearnings. That which you are ashamed of may be exactly that for which you yearn. Here's an example.

Vanessa Jeronne is the poster girl for codependency. Sweet to the point of being syrupy, giving but never taking, Vanessa feels bad whenever she strays from taking care of others. That's a big reason she's been in a series of relationships with dependent, narcissistic men who've loved her far less than she's loved them. The mere thought of putting herself first makes her uncomfortable, she says. She can't quite describe that bad feeling, though. In fact she can't really make herself think about it. All she knows is that long ago she dedicated her life to helping others by sacrificing herself.

Vanessa defends against bad feelings with avoidance, itself a sign of shame. But, if Vanessa could attend to her thoughts and feelings, she'd soon run directly into even more shame in the form of messages like: "You're not good for anything. Nobody wants you. The only way you'll ever be acceptable is if you take care of people." And only then, if she could challenge her shame, would she finally discover her yearnings: to have a life of her own, to meet her own needs, to be in a relationship with someone who responds to her wants and needs.

Excessive shame, then, both attacks your yearnings and tells you that you have them. That means that sometimes instead of hiding in avoidance, you must journey through the desert of shame in order to reach the promised land of your yearnings.

Reconnecting with Your Yearnings

Here are some steps you can take to start on that path through the desert. The goals are to get through the badlands, discover your yearnings, and decide what to do with them.

- Use your shame to identify your yearnings.
- Reclaim your right to yearn.
- Reclaim your specific yearnings.
- Decide how you will honor your yearnings now and in the future.

Use Your Shame to Identify Your Yearnings

There are two good ways to use shame to help you identify your yearnings. The first is to think carefully about this phrase: "I want _____, but _____." Exactly what do you want in life that you keep deferring? Do you feel something you might call shame or guilt when you think about actually getting whatever it is? Does it somehow seem to you you have no right to get whatever fills that mysterious blank following the word "want"?

The second way is to make a list of your "shoulds" and especially of your "shouldn'ts." Your "shoulds" are your obligations and expectations such as "I should always be there for my children" and "I should work twelve hours a day." They are the things you are supposed to do with your life whether or not you really want to. Those "shouldn'ts" represent prohibitions, all the wants and needs and drives and wishes that you are supposed to refute. People usually obey their shoulds and shouldn'ts because of the fear of feeling shame if they don't.

It's also helpful to note the many areas where shame can drive your wants into hiding. Shame can become attached to specific feelings such as fear or anger, so that you feel shame at the very moment when you begin to feel those emotions. The person who feels shame simultaneously with anger will quickly learn to hide that anger even from the self so as to avoid the shame. Shame can even cling to the feeling of joy, so that someone renounces their right to feel good about themselves or about life. People can also become "shame bound" about having any feelings at all. These persons must attempt to cut off all their emotions lest they become overwhelmed with feelings of shameful weakness.

But feelings aren't the only things you can be shamed out of. Excessive shame can threaten premature extinction of your drives. All your hungers can be adversely affected, including your attitude toward food in a society that applauds paper-thin models and condemns any hint of heaviness. The need to rest may also become shame bound, producing the kind of nonstop workers so valued in bee hives and American cities. And, certainly, shame's effects upon sexuality are well known. Shame can practically destroy the sex drive in either gender. We'll write later in more detail about how shame affects body image and sexuality.

Interpersonal relationships is another area where shame deeply affects people. Excessive shame can cut people off from their own interpersonal needs, including the desire to nurture others and to accept others' caring, the need for touch and holding, the need to identify and model yourself after another, and the right to be different than others.

Gershen Kaufman (1996) mentions one other shame area particularly important to this discussion about yearnings. He notes that excessive shame often invades the area of purpose and meaning. For example, imagine what would happen if a girl's parents laughed or sneered whenever she mentioned wanting to become a minister. Her dream of purpose, her sense of how she could best contribute to the world, would be crushed. She might even push that dream far into the recesses of her mind so as not to feel again the shame of having her dreams of goodness held up for ridicule.

So think about your shame. What yearnings does it hide? What follows the "I want . . ."? What shoulds and shouldn'ts keep you from knowing your real wants and needs? What major areas of your life have been prohibited so that only a vague feeling of shame remains?

Reclaim Your Right to Yearn

You can't reclaim any particular yearning until you reclaim the more general *right* to yearn. That means making a commitment to listen to dreams, to daydream, and to take the time really to think about what matters most. This step is especially critical for those readers whose shame is connected with purpose, meaning, choice, and higher pursuits. If you grew up being told that you should just do as you were told and not ask questions, that you should keep your nose to the grindstone, that you should aim for security rather than adventure, that being good means doing what your parents or others do instead of listening to your own heart, then you need to give yourself permission now to yearn.

It's not easy to yearn when shame interferes. One clue is that your mind tries to shift away from "bigger" thoughts whenever they come up. You might get uncomfortable if someone asks you anything important about yourself. It's easier to switch the subject than answer those kinds of questions because they frighten you. Nor can you grapple with the meaning of your life when you're alone. Even then your shame accompanies you, telling you just to shut up and watch the movie or make supper or keep busy somehow.

The point is that you have the right to yearn. Only you can reclaim that right from your shame, though. You have to want it back enough to refuse to be distracted when your shame tries to push you away from your dreams.

Reclaim Your Specific Yearnings

Once you have reclaimed the right to yearn, you are ready to discover what you most yearn for. Perhaps you know the answer clearly by now just by having gone through the first two steps above, but maybe not. Yearnings are pretty elusive, after all, even when you've given yourself permission to notice them. True, you may have to go into a darkened field at night in order to have a chance to see a shooting star. But, usually, you still have to wait awhile even after you get there before one appears.

Here are several questions you can ask yourself that will help you discover your so far hidden yearnings:

- "What do I wish I had the guts to do with my life that so far I have avoided?"

- "What would give my life greater meaning?"

- "What do I yearn for?"

- "What would I do if it weren't for the fear of others' disapproval?"

- "How could I contribute to the world in ways that would really feel right?"

- "What do I dream about? What do I daydream about?"

Please note that reclaiming your yearnings doesn't necessarily mean renouncing all that you have done with your life so far. That's simply not necessary, because you've probably done a lot of good just as you are. It's far more likely that yearnings will offer opportunities to add to your life rather than taking anything away. For instance, a baker who reclaims her yearning to develop her spiritual self may do so through prayer and good works without having to quit the bakery. On the other hand, that baker might indeed decide to change careers. Sometimes yearnings do lead to sea changes in people's lives.

Honoring Your Yearnings

The fourth step in this process is to honor your yearnings. The question here is what, specifically, are you willing and able to do that is consistent with what you yearn for. This can be a difficult step. It's so much easier to talk about living in certain ways than actually to live that way—as anyone who has ever attempted to "eat healthy" almost certainly knows.

The formula is this:

Since I yearn for _____, I commit to _____ with my life.

Since I yearn for personal peace, I commit to quit looking for things to be angry about in life and begin searching for the positive.

Since I yearn to create, I commit to take an "artist day" once a week (Cameron, 1992).

Since I yearn to wander and discover, I commit to saving up for a trip to India next year.

Since I yearn for knowledge, I commit to reading three serious books this summer.

Since I yearn for spiritual contentment, I commit to learning how to meditate.

Honoring yearnings, obviously, is not something done in the abstract. It demands a commitment of time and energy. But that time will feel especially well spent if these are your true yearnings. Pursuing your yearning will help you feel connected with yourself at the deepest level of your being.

One way to honor your yearnings is to let out the creative part of you. You're probably most creative when you play, dream, and brainstorm—when you put all your "shoulds" and "shouldn'ts" on the shelf for a while, along with your shame, so that you can sense all your opportunities in life without immediate judgement.

It's strange how shame both keeps people away from their yearnings and acts as a guide to find them. It does do both, though, and does them well.

Exercises

1. Yearnings are deep longing feelings that you may have learned to ignore or to suppress as "impractical," "inappropriate," "silly," "impossible," "crazy," or "unreachable." Perhaps you have some

other words that you use to push your yearnings away—or perhaps you avoid thinking about your yearnings at all. Keep a small notebook in your pocket or purse for the next month or two and jot down all the ideas or wishes that you usually push away. Even if you're not used to thinking about your deepest desires, try to relax your mind and let your yearnings flow, writing them in your notebook when you get a moment. Don't judge what you write down. At the end of a month, read your notes over and see if there are one or more ideas, wants, wishes, journeys, or yearnings in your notebook that might be important to you, no matter *how* impractical, inappropriate, silly, impossible, unrealistic, or crazy your logical self tells you they are. Let yourself dream about those a bit more. Who knows? They may take you where you most want to go. Talk some of them over with a friend who has a good imagination and understands you.

2. Imagine yourself sitting on a white disc about eight feet across. This disc is a "free space" for thinking, dreaming, and eventually planning. You can look in all directions from the center of this disc. You may look up and down. You may look north and south, east and west. And you can look inside, as well as in all the other outside directions. Take as much time as you need in the next few days, stopping to sit and to look in each direction. As you do so, ask yourself what you would most like to have in your life, what kind of work you would most like to do in the world and for the world, and what your directions are about how you can bring your yearnings into fruition in your life.

3. Most people have wanted to belong to something, and most of them also have been afraid to join some group. One person we know had always felt that she could never belong because she didn't have anything to contribute to most groups. When she was asked to join one anyway, she had to think very hard for a couple of months to find something she had that was worth giving to others. Finally, she found one thing she believed she could help another group member do, and she was able to tell herself that, because of this, there was room in the group for her. Of course, the space for her had been there the whole time, but she wasn't able to accept it until she had found a reason for self-esteem. While she now feels that she belongs, everyone else has been gifted by her presence, and everyone else in the group knows that she has the kind of heart they will always welcome. What contributions could you make to a group if you didn't let your shame or fear of shame stop you from joining and speaking up?

4. Cut out two paper hearts about four inches tall and three to four inches wide. Match them together and glue around the bottom and side edges, leaving an opening at the top. Take another piece of paper and write your name on it. Light a candle, put the paper with your name on it inside your heart, and blow out the candle. Put the heart in your pocket or purse to remind you that you need to practice putting yourself in your own heart in order to hear your yearnings.

5. Begin a dream journal. Set a notebook and pencil by your bed and tell yourself as you go to sleep that you will remember your dreams. It may take a couple of weeks before it works, so don't give up too soon. When you awake, go over the dream in your mind before you move; when you have done that, sit up and write it in your notebook. Notice that after a while if you ask your dreams to reveal your yearnings to you, they will begin to do that.

Creative
Approaches to
Healing Shame

Beginning to Heal Your Shame

Now that you've learned all about what shame is and have some ideas about where your shame may have come from, you're ready to begin tapping your creativity to begin to heal your shame. But, even armed with all of your new knowledge, we can't promise that your healing journey will be easy—just necessary. Healing the wounds of shame is sometimes more difficult than healing other emotional injuries. One reason shame is so hard to heal is that people run away from shame in many ways. For example, try imagining that your shame is like a physical problem—like an ulcer, for instance. Now, you can't heal an ulcer by pretending it doesn't exist; even if quits bothering you for a while, it will still be there and still get worse. You may find yourself avoiding doctors because seeing them reminds you that you're avoiding your health problem. To avoid facing the situation, you may be tempted to blame your ulcer on other people. But, blaming your ulcer on other people certainly won't heal it. It will just make getting along with people more of a strain, and that could exacerbate your ulcer even more. Being angry with yourself or your body because it made the ulcer won't help either. Being angry about a problem doesn't make it go away. Pretending that you're better than people with ulcers might help hide that you have one, but it won't help heal it.

These strategies may sound pretty silly. After all, everyone knows that in order to heal an ulcer you have to pay some attention to the ulcer itself. But, as silly as they seem, these are the kinds of things people do in order to "get rid" of their shame. Sometimes people believe that if they just block shame from their conscious awareness, it really will go away. They pretend the shame or shaming situation doesn't exist. They avoid other people, places, and situations that might bring the shame to the surface of their minds. They blame others for their own discomfort. Sometimes shamed people get angry at the folks they're blaming, doing and saying things that only make them more ashamed later. They can get angry with themselves and make their situations much worse by heaping scorn upon themselves for reacting angrily or for feeling shame at all. They try to prove themselves worthy of respect in ways that don't produce respect—but can produce resentment, disgust, and fear in others. They hurt those others and hurt themselves in those relationships.

People are so good at defending themselves from their own feelings of shame that they don't really see the need of facing that shame and working through it. You may know that feeling angry, hopeless, and numb doesn't help you heal, but also that it may feel better temporarily than facing your shame. Facing shame means thinking about it, feeling it, sorting through what's true and not true about it. Healing shame takes time and energy, and looking at shame directly is painful. Often people feel that it's so painful that they simply can't do it. They can run into trouble when they try to get help and discover that many traditional methods of therapy require that these issues be faced "head on."

Another problem shamed people may discover is that traditional therapy is centered around talking, and putting the experience of shame into words isn't easy. It's even harder when you're speaking directly to another person whom you respect and whom you want to think well of you. Healing shame can mean talking about things that you wish hadn't occurred in the past or didn't occur now. It means "confessing" to events in your life (whether you were responsible or not) that have left you feeling badly about yourself.

You may feel ashamed of sharing so directly. Furthermore, to talk about your experience of shame or the painful memories surrounding that experience may be breaking rules you learned when you were small—rules that told you to hide your weaknesses and pain. One way to ease into talking about painful or shame-filled experiences is to build a nonverbal bridge using your creativity. A creative method that results in product—writing, drawing, sculpting, carving, collage, almost any kind of creative activity can function as an intermediary. You can say to yourself (and another person), "Look! *This* is what it looks like, feels like, and *that* is what happened." And the other person (and you) can look at what you made. That sense of being exposed to prying eyes at a vulnerable time is ameliorated because talking about something painful becomes much easier when you know that someone else already understands what you're going to talk about. With that kind of introduction, you are reassured a little that you won't be completely rejected. And taking the opportunity yourself to look at what you make can give you a little bit of distance. The picture you've drawn may show you how you felt, but it's not how you are feeling right now. So creative methods are powerful in that they can provide a sense of safety and an opportunity to take a step back "to see" your feelings in a different light. These methods can help you feel protected both from rejection from others and (what may be even worse) a rejection of yourself. This sense of safety is a first step in healing your shame.

Heal More Quickly with Creativity

It can be hard to look directly at shame issues without being overwhelmed by uncomfortable feelings. Creative methods can often help you see shame issues with less painful impact. What methods are creative? Any way of looking at, thinking about, or expressing feelings about experiences, ideas, or relationships is creative if it:

- stretches your thinking;

- encourages you to see in a different way;

- helps you question old beliefs or rules;

- leads you past a stuck point to a new learning place.

Methods such as drawing and painting, writing and dancing, acting and playing music are things you might consider "creative." But you don't have to be an artist to create a new vision for yourself. In fact, looking at one thing in a new way, seeing a new meaning and relating it to yourself is an essential part of being creative. Most people do this automatically, without even thinking about it. However, because shame can cut off contact with the world, you may have forgotten how to gain access to your creative abilities. This chapter will help you get back in touch with your creative side, helping you find creative and personal ways to heal your shame.

It's vital that you make use of your creativity, because creative activity can help heal shame more quickly and easily, just like snowshoes will take a person across big drifts of snow. The person still has to make an effort, but getting there is easier and quicker because they don't sink down to the bottom at every step. The snowshoes distribute the weight that is so heavy and keep the person supported and balanced. That way they can walk on top of the drifts. Getting to the same place by the same path is still a journey, but it's an easier one.

The creative is playful, sometimes indirect, and even a little unpredictable and mysterious. That means that the shame work you do will be a journey of discovery, not just slogging through painful understandings until they go away. The mystery is an important part of the journey. Even when you know where you want to go, the path may have surprising twists and turns in it that take your breath away and teach you more than you ever expected.

New Routes to Healing

Healing and being creative are both kinds of growth, and each informs the other, adding strength and structure to the process of becoming whole. This can be seen in many areas. For example, the creative act of learning to dance can be good medicine for weaker ankles. Doing crossword or other pencil puzzles may help a person rebuild brain pathways after the brain has been injured. The puzzles stimulate the brain itself to be creative and to make new pathways where the old ones were erased. Many new activities can challenge you enough to encourage you to move out of the ruts and gain a new view. Seeing things differently is often both creative and healing.

Emotional pain is not always as visible as a physical problem. As a result, it doesn't get talked about as much. Most people struggle with themselves over the emotional pain they have. It's tough to look at their lives and themselves without either becoming ashamed or getting defensive. Shame is painful and powerful, a wily foe that can be hard to dispel. Pictures, words, images, and new ideas provide you with tools that you can use to read and reshape your definitions and feelings about shame. They can give perspective on the experiences of healing shame that may otherwise put you off balance. Healing the emotional pain of shame is a difficult task that demands creativity to diminish the pain and to speed the healing process.

There is another reason that creative approaches make healing easier. People often try to use logic and rational thinking to make sense of the world around them. When they try using logic with shame, however, it doesn't seem to have much impact. That's because shame has little to do with logic—it's primarily *emotional*. Feeling something is more like smelling a flower than it is identifying a flower. Since shame is more sensing than logical thinking, pictures, images, and imagination are powerful tools for working with shame. You can tell yourself that it doesn't make sense to feel as much shame as you do about a particular event. But *telling* yourself about shame—giving yourself logical information—will only help so much. Because logic doesn't speak to feelings very well it can be hard to use logic effectively to influence yourself on the emotional level. The fact that you don't need all that pain and even that you don't deserve it only penetrates so far. Creative methods invite a combination of sensing *and* making sense. Thoughts and feelings working together can help you at a deeper level.

There is a final factor. Trying a creative activity or a new activity requires that, even while you're working through your shame issues, you must also focus on doing or using that new activity. You are often doing and feeling at the same time. When you can do something constructive, you won't feel so helpless, and it becomes more difficult for feelings of shame to overwhelm you. If you begin to feel too badly, you know that you can always use your creative work to direct your feelings toward a positive outcome. If you begin to feel overwhelmed by your creative work, you can always stop and go back to it later, when you're more ready or in a better place emotionally. While feeling shame most often leaves people feeling as if they have no control and little worth, healing shame is an activity that you can direct. Therefore actively and creatively engaging in a healing process can help you feel empowered again.

Other Benefits to Creativity

Being creative includes many kinds of activity, all of which can help you express yourself. You've heard the expression, "A picture is worth a thousand words." Something you create with feeling, whether it's a picture, a collage, a dance, a poem, a photograph, or any other artistic expression is often worth much more than you may assume at first glance. Whatever you creatively produce is an expression of important feelings and thoughts, perhaps even ones you've been afraid or ashamed to ask others about. Just getting them out is a big relief for most people. Sharing what you have created with another person helps a lot too. Shame heals best when it's exposed in a safe environment.

Some people just feel safer sharing what they need to share about their shame issues with a piece of music, poetry, or a picture than they do with talking. Being comfortable is very important when you're addressing uncomfortable material like shame feelings and shaming thoughts.

Creative methods also involve more of the total "you" in the healing process, because both the right and left parts of the brain have to be active. Even if all you draw are stick figures, or you're simply cutting out magazine pictures, creativity allows more of your brain to be engaged in the healing process. That means that you can be in a different kind of contact with yourself than usual, that more of your personal resources are engaged in solving the problem, and that there is a greater chance for real change—a change that affects the whole you.

Of course, humor is often creative, too, and can be enormously helpful in the healing process. Luckily, any kind of creative activity opens the door to humor. Play, humor, and fun are all possible and encouraged when you're being creative. These lighter aspects of your emotional range can, in themselves, act as an antidote to shame because they really help you feel better at the time, creating an openness to your having more pleasant feelings and fewer shamed ones. For example, once you put a brown paper bag over your head for a half hour to represent how it feels when you walk around inside of your shame, all you'll have to do is remember it. Then just imagine yourself being wherever you are (in your office at work, grocery shopping) wearing that bag at that moment. Chances are the image will be quite humorous (finally!), and you won't really have to put the bag on again to change your perspective.

Once in a while, everyone gets stuck. Lots of times your thoughts come in words, so it can be a big order to break your mindset and experience something in a new way. For example, suppose that every time you think of yourself as good enough, you begin to feel shame. The feeling and the words are linked so tightly that you can't separate them. But, if you drew a picture of yourself feeling good enough, that picture might take you past the stuck point. You could "see" yourself feeling good enough, even if thinking it was still very difficult. Or let's say that you feel "alien!" and like you don't belong. In order to research what that word "alien" means to you, you could go out and buy a stuffed kid's toy in the shape of an alien. When you got it home, something would have changed. Whether you really noticed it or not, part of your brain would know immediately that now there were *two* "aliens" in the house, and you would no longer be alone. It might take a while for your conscious self to realize this, but chances are that your whole self would go to work on your belonging issues, not just the logical part of your mind. Since the aliens would "belong" together, that other part of you (your right brain) would help you learn more about yourself through that ersatz alien. Many times we have seen people have this kind of experience to a life-changing degree, though many of them didn't share it with us right away because it felt "silly." New behavior and new experiments do feel odd at the beginning, But the act of allowing oneself to be silly instead of ashamed is a way of healing some unnecessary shame and accepting and appreciating yourself as a many-faceted creature. Being creative and possibly silly is in itself a way of getting out of a rut and being uniquely yourself. Knowing at many levels that it's all right to be yourself is a major part of healing the wounds of shame.

Everyone Can Be Creative

A lot of people believe that they aren't creative and don't even have the capacity to be creative. Part of the problem is how "being creative" is defined. Because creativity goes with curiosity and curiosity can get a person into trouble at times, our society may shame people who are very creative. Creativity in our culture is often marked "reserved for artists," who are supposed to be a little odd and eccentric anyway. While a little creativity is encouraged, having a creative perspective on life often is not. We remember visiting a third-grade classroom where the teacher was extremely proud of all the children's art work because all of the turkeys the children had made for Thanksgiving looked remarkably alike. Another time, when our kids decided to color and paint, we decided we would try it with them. Everyone's pictures went up on the wall, but it seemed the visitors always pointed to *our* pictures when they said, "Oh, did your kids draw those?" That could seem discouraging—and even unintentionally shaming. Should adults draw if they can't draw well? And the answer is an unreserved "Yes!" because it helps you express yourself, because you will learn from yourself while doing it, and because diving in and actually doing something is often the best way to learn how to do it.

In reality, almost everyone has the ability to be creative—to see things in new ways, to express themselves in colors and shapes and sounds. One thing that's important about being creative is not to judge so much. When businesspeople are looking for ways to solve a problem, they may "brainstorm" with others. That means everyone says their ideas without censoring them; no matter how silly they sound, everyone agrees not to judge the ideas as good or bad. All ideas are allowed and examined for what is helpful in them. This is the approach we suggest toward using creative methods in order to help heal yourself. Where sham is full of judgment, being creative requires that you learn to leave such judgments behind for a while And we suggest that you not compare your work to anyone else's. First, comparing is an old self-shaming technique that you've probably used for years. Secondly, it isn't fair to yourself to compare. What comes out of you in words or notes or paint is what *needs* to come out. And people need to express very different things when they are doing emotional work. One of the stages recognized in children's painting is one where the child mixes all the colors into a mess, and the picture comes out as a big brownish blob. If you are frustrated and confused, you may need to draw like that; another time, you will make something or write something that is more sophisticated with finer points. The idea is that comparing and judging will only stop you from finding out who you are. Comparing is research to see if you're good enough, and judging is a determination whether you've made it to that standard. Both increase shame, and both stop people from learning about their own abilities to be creative.

Using creative methods to help yourself in working with your shame is optional. It is never something you *have* to do. It's not bad if you pass on trying any of the methods we will discuss here. Using those methods is an invitation to yourself, not another requirement on which to judge yourself. You can think of creativity as a gift to yourself, a way that you can say, "Here, Self, I'm going to give you a little extra space and freedom you can use to help yourself." There will be many choices offered in the rest of this chapter. Help yourself to those that intrigue or touch you. As they say in AA, "Take what you need and leave the rest."

How Can You Be Creative

In the rest of this chapter, we will discuss many possible ways to work with creative methods. In some areas, we may suggest many possibilities. In other areas that you consider creative, there may be no specific suggestions. That doesn't mean that creative activity in those areas may not be useful; probably it would be. Perhaps you can figure out how to draw on the power of your creativity in that area to help yourself. To be valuable, a method has to help you in one, some, or all of the following ways: it must help you understand your shame better, express your shame in some way, challenge your shame in some way, help you break through your shame to do something you couldn't before, or help you see yourself or the world in a new way—as good, good enough, belonging, lovable, needed, special, unique, or all of those things. Healing shame isn't easy, and it means learning for yourself that being human means making some mistakes and correcting the ones you need to correct as best you can. You will also learn about feelings such as pride, independence, sadness, curiosity, anger, forgiveness, compassion, gratitude, and self-caring. Your creativity can help you discover these feelings in many different ways.

For example, at fifty-seven Nancy felt ashamed of herself because, as she grew older, she got sick and couldn't move very well. She had especially loved to dance in the past, but she didn't even have the money to go watch dancing now. She felt like there was something wrong with her because she could find no way to connect herself to the arts that she had loved. However, Nancy did have a camera. She gave herself an "assignment" to go walking outside and take pictures of anything she saw "dancing." She returned with a handful of pictures of trees and flowers she had caught moving gracefully. She felt as if she had been part of a dance in taking the pictures. And, in spite of her current reduced economic status, she became a volunteer, helping with the community arts center and theater. Her self-esteem improved. She had rejoined society as a member of a community. She no longer felt defective, but instead as if she was an insightful and adequate person—which is, of course, what she was. Even though this may not be what she originally thought of as a "creative" act, such as drawing or painting, it turned out to be powerfully creative, helping her remove a great deal of emotional pain and shame from her daily life.

The Value of Journaling

Using a journal is a creative way to keep track of what you have done, what you are doing now, and what your progress is like. Beginning a journal isn't difficult. It's making sure that you get back to it and writing somewhat regularly that can be tricky. What you write doesn't have to be complicated. It can be a description of something that happened today that triggered your shame or your pride. Or it could be a dialogue between conflicting ideas and feelings. Here is a sample of a recent entry from Maya's "Shame/Pride Journal."

> When Chance complimented me, today, I could feel myself blushing. Just for a minute, I felt like I used to feel and I wanted to disappear. But I took a deep breath in and out, and I didn't just back away. I could even thank him without stuttering. And when he left the lunchroom, I felt okay about the way I had acted. It wasn't like I usually feel—stupid, because I was shy and ran away. This is really a big change for me, and it does feel better. I feel more grown-up and like a normal woman.

And here is another sample, this time taken from Jay-Jay's journal dialogue between his "handsome self" and "ugly self."

Ugly: No wonder people look at you funny. Your sideburns don't even match.

Handsome: You're always criticizing something. Maybe people look at me because they like what they see. Or because I know how to have fun, and because I like people.

Ugly: Oh, sure! Or because you're the Easter bunny! Look at that zit on your nose. Who wouldn't stare at the thing? When will you get it through your head that you're never gonna look good enough for anybody to love you? They'll only laugh behind your back. You are too ugly for this world, Jay-Jay.

Handsome: I used to feel like that stuff you say. But I can hardly see that zit. Everybody gets them. I refuse to feel bad about that. You just want me to feel bad about myself like I used to. But I'm beginning to like the way I look and I don't feel so bad anymore—and I'm getting tired of you. Cut it out and go away unless you have something important to tell me.

Clearly, the process of healing shame is no smoother than the healing of physical wounds. Sometimes it's simple, and other times there are complications. Some wounds have poison in them. Whenever a person has been quite injured, the healing process is likely to take longer and have some ups and downs. It's useful to have some record of the healing process so that repeated patterns can be identified. That's why your doctor keeps a chart on you. That chart makes it possible to see what helps and what doesn't, what your temperature was last time and what it is today, and what has worked to return you to a healthy temperature in the past.

The journal is one of the best tools we have found to accomplish something similar when you're healing shame. We are talking about a personal journal in which you describe your own experience for yourself. It can be especially helpful if you are willing to write without censoring yourself, and if you're willing to allow yourself to draw and doodle in it as well as write. There are three people who are excellent at describing different ways of using your journal and the process of keeping track of yourself in journals. They are Julia Cameron (1992), Lucia Cappachione (1979), and Natalie Goldberg (1998). If you need help getting started, their books are listed in our References section.

But you can begin on your own as well. Just write. Just draw. Be honest with yourself, and do your best to go beyond complaining. When you have a beautiful moment, include that. If you are actively healing your shame, you are changing the balance of your thoughts and feelings to include many more positive experiences. These are just as important as the ones that leave you feeling defective or inadequate.

Different Ways to Use Your Journal

We could encourage you to use your journal as a way of expressing feelings, communicating with yourself at any level and showing yourself things about you, as well as a place for recording things that you may want or need to remember. Here are some ideas about ways to write in your journal so it can act in these specific ways and begin to help you face and heal your shame.

Write yourself letters to think about. If you are a shamed person, you spend plenty of time on what other people think. But do you ever consider what you think? Write some of these letters when you are feeling good as well as when you're not. Answer the letters you write to yourself. Establish a dialogue about your own life that goes beyond the words "should" and "should not." Play both parts of any conflict instead of shoving some parts of yourself away.

Make a list of the things that others do or say against those people they don't like. Then write a letter to yourself about the mean things you do and say about yourself. Make a commitment to change at least one behavior and write about the changes in the journal as time goes on.

Make up stories about the world: what you would really like to have happen in your life, what the birds outside your window seem to be saying as they sing, how that weed in the corner of the yard managed to grow taller than any of the flowers, what your imaginary dog said to you today. Be imaginative. Write stories about what you did the day you awoke and every piece of clothing you owned was missing (an experience of exposure, for sure), or about the time your head swelled up so big it completely popped like a balloon and how, ever since, you have been able to accept all of the compliments people give you because you've already survived your worst fear about having too much pride (an antidote to being afraid that good things will make you bad).

Be downright open with yourself and write down all those ideas you hesitate to tell anyone else. If you had the power to change just one thing in the world, what would you choose to change? What secret bothers you the most and why? What secret need do you have? If you invented something to meet that secret need, what would it be? What would you do with three wishes? How do you feel about what you would do with them? If you were an animal, what kind of animal would you be and why? What do you really think and feel about the things that are happening in your life? Does a computer remind you more of a math lesson or a ouija board? How come? Openness to yourself is important in a lot of ways. First, getting to know yourself is important and you don't have to begin where you are most fearful. Second, being open with yourself about your own feelings and ideas without judging them is an antidote to self-shaming. Third, openness and play are the foundation of creating and accepting new things. That doll that rides up in the front seat of a person's car so human predators won't know that you're driving alone was once a "silly" idea. So was a robot vacuum cleaner, crash-test dummy, better can opener (and we can still work on that one), and the telephone. Giving yourself freedom to write in any way gives you broader freedom to think, to feel, and to put different kinds of things together in new ways to make your emotional life happier and easier.

Write down the shame episodes you experience as they occur. Write them in detail, if it will help you figure out what triggered them. Write down anything that might help you understand about where or when that particular kind of shame originated in your life. Ask yourself how you might behave and feel if you did not have shame of that particular kind. Do you want to soften the shame you have or get rid of all of it? Is this kind of shame helpful in any way or is it just so painful or excessive that it's not helpful at all? Does your experience change as time goes on? What could you try to give your-self more confidence or faith in yourself?

Make up some mantras for yourself while you are entering things in your journal. A mantra is a statement that you say over and over again to focus your own attention: "I am lovable," or "Shame fades and pride grows tall." When you wake up not feeling so good, find one of them to carry with you all that day. "I am perfectly human," is another good example, in case you happen to be a perfectionist.

Put some music on while you write and see where it takes you. Can you find music that makes you automatically shift your thinking and feeling from shame to strength? If you track your music experi-ences in your journal, soon you will have developed a record of what relieves you and what makes your pain worse. Then you can start making clearer choices about a whole new aspect of your fife. For example, one woman felt very sad, angry, and ashamed when her boyfriend left her. After a whole year of feeling miserable, she went to a counselor who asked her what kind of music she was listening to. Well, it was all sad songs that dealt with rejection—which was what she felt ashamed about. The counselor had this client's two kids come in and asked them to demand their mother change the station any time one of those songs came on. The kids were more than happy to do that. In fact, sometimes they changed the stations them-selves. They were tired of sad songs, and they wanted a happier mother. In two weeks the mom's depression, sadness, and shame at being rejected were really reduced. She was listening to different music and experiencing her life in a different way. When she took a good look at it, she was pleased that she had not gotten trapped in that relationship, since it wouldn't have been very good for her after all. This illustrates how powerful music can be, and what you can learn from yourself in ways that you don't even imagine and in ways that you don't recognize. When you find music to nurture you, it can help you move through your emotions, including shame.

Make lists in your journal. Make a "should" list and then go back over it, changing all the "shoulds" to "coulds." Then write how it feels for these things to be "coulds," things you have choices about and can do or not do. Make a list of what you're proud of, even if you have to think a long time and you start with just one thing. Make a list of the names you will give the twelve children you will have in an alternative universe, and why you choose those names. Make another list of what you will feel most proud of in them as they grow up. Make a list of all the really reasonable meals you have eaten in the past week. Evaluate that list and propose any changes that would add to your self-care. List all of the things you would do with your time if you had no "shoulds" to do. Then number those things in priority of what is most to least important to you. Write down how long it has been since you have done each of them, or if you have never done some of them. Make another blank list and add them as you begin to do these things for yourself.

Write letters to others. Write all the things you would like to say but can't yet, or things you would feel too ashamed to say. Get those thoughts and feelings out on paper. Remember that shame heals when it is exposed in a safe environment, and that reading those thoughts and feelings over will help you to take one step back and look more clearly at them. Make your journal a safe place for you to share by not judging yourself. The more accepting you are of yourself, the more and deeper information you will begin to share with yourself on a conscious level.

Use your imagination in giving yourself assignments for your journal. If you were a tree—just one tree—what kind of tree would you be and why? Starting in the summer, write about that tree as it survives all the seasons, going all the way through fall, winter, and spring. Ask yourself if there are any comparisons to how you yourself have survived the seasons of shame in your life. Or, take time once a week to reread the last week's writing. Then change pens and let "Dr. Wisdom" (the one inside) write back to you and give you any advice that's needed. Don't be too surprised if Dr. Wisdom gives pretty sound advice with a sense of humor.

Write a letter to yourself apologizing when you have failed to take good care of yourself. Write a letter to your shaming self, accepting it and suggesting that the two of you cooperate to set good boundaries instead of sabotaging each other. Write a letter praising yourself, and over time write thank-you's to yourself for the good things you're doing until you learn how to praise and thank yourself just as you might another person.

Use your journal as a resource that you turn to when you're confused, as something that helps you be there for yourself, as a friend who offers good options when it's hard to think of any at the time, and as a record of your growth and healing. Every six months, re-read some of it to make sure that you haven't fallen back into the old shame and shaming habits, but that you're continuing to grow. This will help you catch yourself if you get off track.

If you are hesitant to write in your journal because you're afraid someone will read it without your permission, remember that you can use drawing or collage for some entries in your journal. You can use your own word code for things you wish to keep private. Everyone has a right to privacy.

The Value of Drawing and Painting

You can also use drawing and painting to help you in your healing process. You don't have to be an artist to use lines or shapes or color to express what you feel. Elena decided to try drawing because she had so much trouble finding words to use to help her. She used Magic Markers so she could draw whenever and wherever she felt like drawing. One day she decided to make a picture of her shame. As she put it, "It wasn't until then that I understood how heavy shame felt to me. It was like a huge iron weight pressing down on my head and shoulders, so I couldn't raise my head. It was so big and heavy and black that I could hardly stand. But I was still hanging on to it, making sure it didn't fall off my shoulders. That picture helped me see how I oppress myself." Rocky had an entirely different experience when he drew his shame. He said, "At first nothing came to me. I was stumped about what my shame might look like, but then I started drawing eyes. There were eyes all over in my picture. It was as if I were being stared at all the time, and I couldn't hide. That was always what I felt like at home. Mama was always so sure that I was going to do something bad that I didn't have any privacy at all. She would even knock on the bathroom door and ask what I was doing if I was in there more than two minutes. One of the first things I did was hang that picture up, facing the wall, so those eyes couldn't see anything anymore. It was a big relief to know why I was always feeling under scrutiny. Turning the picture to the wall helped me realize I didn't have to treat myself that way all the time, examining everything I do to find out what's bad and wrong about it." It's clear that for Elena and Rocky drawing pictures of their shame helped them understand themselves.

Drawing and painting can help you connect with the goodness inside you, too; it can help you find yourself, or discover that parts of you that you've pushed away are actually good things that you could cherish, instead. And it can help you by simply expressing the nature of what you cannot say to yourself yet. Lines and color provide relief and insight. When you're not sure how to put something or what to say to describe how you are feeling, draw or color a picture of how you feel.

Shamed persons are often intimidated by the thought of doing anything "artistic" because they feel sure that they "won't do it right." But the truth about what we're discussing here is that *you can't do it wrong*. First, the picture is an expression of your feelings, not something that is supposed to be artful or even realistic. Secondly, it is *yours* and no one else's. It doesn't have to be compared to anything. Judging your drawing only stops the process of healing. Letting yourself be who you are without rejecting yourself is a substantial part of healing shame. If your drawings are unformed it may be because the feelings come from a time when you were younger. Or, it could be that you have felt ashamed for so long that you never gave yourself the opportunity to practice expressing yourself.

If you are still telling yourself that you cannot draw or color anything right, start using crayons to draw or paint with fingerpaints. Nobody can draw very well with crayons or paint the Sistine Chapel with fingerpaints. Since it's nearly impossible to be really artistic with these media, you won't have to worry how your pictures look. Just experiment. If you are self-conscious about anyone seeing you draw, try drawing with sidewalk chalk in big parking lots where everyone can see you, bringing your kids with you to draw, too. Other people will assume you're out there for the children, so there will be less pressure about being seen while you let yourself get used to drawing.

If drawing and painting are just too much for you, you can do lots of the same things with collage. Just cut pictures out of magazines and paste them together on cardboard until you have completed doing what you set out to do or until you have simply expressed what you're feeling. Here's another collage exercise to try: Take a square cardboard box apart and collage both the inside and the outside. On what will be the outside, put pictures of how you show yourself to others. On what will be the inside when you fold it back up, collage what is inside you, including your shame. Then fold the box back up to see how it has come out. Your goal, if you are healing shame is to slowly begin to expose the shamed feelings until you don't need to hide those feelings from yourself or others, and the painful feelings begin to be replaced by other feelings.

Different Ways to Use Drawing and Painting

Here are some things you can do with drawing or painting that may be of help to you in learning about yourself and beginning to feel better related to shame and shame issues.

- Draw a picture of how you feel when you are being shamed by someone else, or how you felt in a particular situation. Find out what colors feel most like your shame to you, and what kinds of shapes or images. You may wish to draw other feelings, too, like sadness, anger, or paranoia. Put your drawings up somewhere if you can, until you really get to know them. Sometimes you will notice important things later that you hadn't seen at first.

- Draw things the way you would have liked to see them instead of the way they really were. If your father was very critical or distant, draw him happier and closer to you. Revision your world. It's a way of taking some power back in terms of the way you look at life.

- If you're a person who is ashamed of other feelings as well as shame, draw them again and again until you have accepted them into your life. They are parts of you, and you need not be ashamed of your feelings. Let yourself think of your life and experiences in a more humane way through your drawings.

- Draw a series of pictures to show yourself walking down a path, finding your shame, figuring out how to deal with it, and going on to what is next in your life.

- Draw your heart. If it needs mending in some way, figure out how you can mend it. Then draw a picture of how you are proud of your mended heart and the wonderful things that your heart has given you.

- Draw or make a shield that you can use to protect yourself from other people's shaming. Put your strengths on it and put it on the wall where you will see it when you need it.

- Draw the vulnerable inner self that you abandoned, and find out what it needs from you today—this very day. Give it that, if you can.

- Draw one tree every night before you go to bed. Make the tree represent how you felt that day. Look back after one day and see how the days were different. Can you tell which days you had to struggle more with shame. Look back over them again at the end of thirty days. Your thirty trees will probably show you your patterns and feelings pretty clearly. What do they say about how the way in which you use your shame helps or hinders you?

Remember that there are no set rules for what kinds of pictures are good or bad to draw. You might find an important part of you that needs nurturing or attention in one of your pictures. On the other hand, a picture could just look plain ugly and still be meaningful. One woman was feeling very ugly herself. She decided that the only way she could paint that day without feeling even worse about herself was to paint the most ugly picture she could manage, on purpose. Then, if her picture was really ugly, she would still have accomplished her assignment and could be proud of having done it. Besides, the ugliest thing she could think of would really be just the way she felt. Well, she did paint ugliness and it was *very* ugly, and she felt a whole lot better when she was done. To her surprise, she had painted a lot of ugliness right out of her feelings and into that painting. She felt really relieved, and she threw the yucky painting in a corner of the basement. A few years later one of her kids found it and hung it on his wall, to her horror. He refused to take it down, and when he heard his mom had painted it, he told his friends. For some reason, that ugly painting let him know that it was okay to feel the way he did during that part of his adolescence. Eventually he grew out of that phase and threw the picture back in the basement. The woman learned that drawings and paintings don't have to look good to be meaningful, and that even the most painful feelings can be shared in some ways.

The Value of Working with Clay

Working through your shame is a fascinating journey at times, and full of mystery. There may be times when a "hands on" approach is required and you may find that clay is the best way to explore and to express yourself. Clay has some special properties for work in this area. In many ways, working with clay unwraps what you have hidden from yourself. Sometimes that can be a magic step in healing shame. Shame is a resistant emotion and people can sometimes be stubborn about changing. The toughness of the clay often functions as a symbol of your own resistance. It takes energy and hard work to wrestle with the clay, and because it does, you may break through old pieces of your resistance that really aren't needed anymore. Clay is also something that can keep changing, instead of something static that forever after stays exactly that way. Because shame is often a stuck point, part of being in a rut, the ability to continue to reshape the clay can become really important in your own effort to transcend the ruts and get to more level ground. And clay is representative of another thing you may be doing as well: with clay, you make a mess and get your fingers dirty; with clay you also clean up your own mess, putting things "back into shape."

Clay is, in a manner of speaking, what people are made of. Like human beings, it's messy and its colors may bleed and it may not turn into the perfect form you had in mind. Of course, when people are doing healing work, nobody's clay is really supposed to be artistic, so you don't need to worry about doing things "right." There is no wrong way to work with your clay. What you will make of your clay is what it's supposed to be. You really are just giving your less conscious side a better opportunity to speak with you. If you allow that to happen, you will get a message of sorts. Sometimes you'll know right away what it is, and at other times you may have to mull it over. But even when it is at its most difficult, the clay will be a helpful friend.

To do the best shame work you will need to have the tougher resistance of either plasticine or self-hardening hobby clay. Plasticine comes in rectangular packages and can be found in most toy stores and some variety stores at less expense than in art supply stores. But art supply plasticine often comes in a much wider range of colors. Either one will do. Self-hardening clay usually is found in hobby stores or art supply stores. It is more like the clay used to make pots that can be kilned, and comes only in gray or brick red in most places. It may cost more than plasticine, because it comes in at least five-pound packages. You can make something from it and let it dry—though it can get crumbly if not handled carefully. You can also make a piece and keep it on a pan under Saran Wrap, with a wet washrag next to it. Under these conditions it stays malleable and you can remold your piece many times. Plasticine stays a little sticky instead of ever drying and can also be remolded for as long you want.

The Process of Claywork

There is a regular process to work with if you are healing shame. Here are some steps you can follow to gain the most from your work.

1. Know that you're going to make at least a small mess, and that making messes is an important part of living. All human beings are messy in some way, and it's okay to get your hands dirty. "Dirty" is a word that describes why some people hide their shame. Now you can bring yours out into the open by making a bit of a mess with good, clean clay.

2. Take a good fifteen minutes to just warm up the clay before you work. You can take as much longer than that as you'd like. In some ways, this is the most important step, because it gives you the opportunity to warm up to working with the clay. You will get along a lot better if you make sure to complete this step.

3. Your main assignment is simple and requires no thinking. Just play with the clay, and let it become what it would like to be. Sometimes it forms right away, sometimes it stays an unclear mass, but play with it for at least a half hour, unless you get the clear message that it is "done." To do this, you will have to listen to yourself and to trust yourself. Listening to yourself like this is a healing process when you are struggling with a lot of shame. In fact, as you learn to trust yourself more deeply again, that shame will subside to a great degree.

4. Now look at what your clay has become. Some people will have a figure of themselves, a figure of a shaming person, a body part, a particular object that has meaning for them, a metaphorical image such as a wall surrounding a small flower, or only a shaped piece of clay that seems mysterious to you. Some people find they have created an image of an experience of shame, such as the Vietnam war veteran whose clay took the shape of himself and a dead buddy sitting on a bench together. He had deep shame over not having been able to save his friend and had felt defective ever since. Now he was ready to let go of that shame and let what he remembered of his buddy back into his life without self-hatred. If you have created a strong image such as this, you know the most important thing you will need to talk to someone about, whether that person is a friend, counselor, pastor, or just God.

5. Just looking at what your clay has become, note any ideas or thoughts you have or memories that come to mind. Then, even if it feels forced, odd, silly, or embarrassing, take the step of pretending that you *are* that lump of clay and talk about yourself or write about yourself as if you were indeed that lump of clay. If you can, tape record what you say so you can listen to it later. This part of the processing, if you allow yourself to do it, is where you will often tell yourself things that surprise you and where you may discover that, in working the clay, you have created a serendipitous figure

that is saying something really important about how you handle your life. Serendipity is a surprising and helpful but unexpected result, a happy occurrence that wasn't logically planned out.

Here are some examples of what others have found:

- **Person 1:** I am a ball made of clay. I am red. I feel all balled up and I can't find out how to open up again. When I try to bounce, I get flat on one side. But if I am really gentle with myself instead of bouncing myself around, I can just roll right across the floor and go anywhere I want to.

- **Person 2:** (Seven-year-old girl) I have two pieces of clay. Here is a little girl and that is me. I have my new barrette in my hair and I look nice. In this piece of clay I am a blue ball with a red spot on it. I am on the world, and the red spot is where the trouble is. I'm glad I did this clay, because I was feeling bad. Everything was all mixed up together. I guess I thought that big red spot of trouble was *me*. But it isn't. I needed to do clay again so that I could remember that the trouble is in the world and not in me.

- **Person 3:** I am a clay woman and my neck is bent almost in half. I can only look at the ground, and I am sad and lonely. I feel like this happened to me a long time ago, but I still can't lift up my head. I feel like I'm stuck but I can't see any way out. Maybe the person who made me out of this clay will have to help me hold my head up.

- **Person 4:** I am yellow and green clay. I look bright and cheerful, but I am in the shape of a big butt. I could be lots of other shapes. But if I took like a big butt, other people will stay away. It's easier, because I don't go around hoping they will like me. The problem is I have lots of energy and I would like to have fun, but being a big butt does keep people away. I wouldn't really mind a change, but I feel stuck.

As you can see from the examples above, what the clay says while you're pretending to be the clay can become pretty interesting. Sometimes it's okay to do this with a friend. You can help each other to keep in role, to be the clay and say "I am." It's not easy, but you may learn more that way. When you start talking about the clay as "it" you're back to analyzing yourself in the same old way rather than experimenting and breaking into new ground.

Who You Are Changes Over Time

One last thing: The clay you hold represents a part of you, since you have invested your energy in it. Let it have a value in your life, at least for now. Whether or not you talk aloud in your clay work, keep your clay figure around. You may have just a lump, but in two weeks when you pick it up again it may become something recognizable much more quickly. Or, as whatever figure it is, it may begin to seem to need little alterations as you yourself change. The person with the clay woman, above, slowly raised the head of that clay woman as she began to feel better about herself. In three months, that clay woman could hold her head up proudly. What might you have done if you were the person who turned himself into a "big butt"? You might decide to let yourself be curious about other people and become a big nose for while to investigate them. Maybe something else after that—perhaps a big foot to walk a new path.

The Value of Images and Metaphors

In the last section, we gave some examples of people finding their own images and metaphors in clay. Even the seven-year-old was able to see and respond to what her clay turned into. Without thinking about it, people often use images and comparisons on a regular basis. You already get ideas from many of the things around you. Simple metaphors are everywhere you are. The meaning of your life is all around you.

Images speak to the entire person. When you say, "My life is like being caught in a revolving door," there is a sense of purposeless movement, of being a little trapped and swept on, of the world being outside of where you are and passing by too quickly to be grasped. That is an image that you can understand with your reason, and one you can feel with your emotions. Could shaming yourself be like being caught in a revolving door? If it were, what would you have to do to change your life, and how could you do that? There are lots of images we connect to shame very immediately, such as, "I could bave died," "I wanted to sink through the floor," "I felt like I was burning up," and "I felt like a pile of garbage." Whatever images you connect with shame, what would happen if you decided to explore the reverse image? For instance, what it would be like to rise back up through the floor and stand proudly. All of your senses are involved in feelings, and often very strongly with shame. Images and metaphors work with your senses and with your potentials.

Images can help you understand the healing process, too. For example, we live in a northern place and have discovered that warming up after being almost frostbitten is a lot like the recovery from shame for someone who has been shamed badly. Here is how the analogy works:

Frostbite	Shame
· physically numb	· emotionally numb
· have to find a warm place	· have to find an accepting (warm) emotional place
· at first nothing changes much	· at first nothing changes much
· odd prickles and tingles occur	· odd sensations and reactions occur
· prickles and tingles become aches	· odd sensations are recognized as feelings
· person gets painful cramps	· person gets painful feelings
· cramps get worse before they get better	· emotional pain gets worse before it gets better
· if person stays inside, pain suddenly leaves	· if person doesn't use escape, pain suddenly relieves
· person has fingers back with full function	· person has all feelings and functions back
· feelings of wellness	· feelings of wellness

What has been especially important about this analogy is that people who've had frostbite know there is a moment when a person warming up and having cramps in their fingers and toes just wants to get them frozen. These people also know that that critical moment happens *just* before everything gets much better. So, the analogy can help you imaging that healing shame is the same way. There may a point where you just want to quit, but you can try to remember that it is soon after that you will begin to feel better. And who wants to have to go through all that all over again?

When we were growing up, we used to play a kid's game with others. It went like this: One person would leave the room and everyone else would pick an object in the room that represented the person who was "it." The entire group would pick only one object and agree on what it meant. Then the person who was "it" returned and had to find out what object had been chosen to represent them by asking questions. They would continue until they also found out why the group thought the object was like him or her. When they had figured it out, it was someone else's turn to be "it." A game such as this is a way of using a metaphor to look at who you are. For example, you might be a coffeepot if you were someone who always had something brewing and whose spouting off tended to get other people active. You could be a book if you were quiet but had lots of information inside, or a comic book if you were a funny person whose life was like a soap opera. You might be a window if you were a person who helped other people see things clearly.

This is a kind of game you can use to help yourself get out of the rut of shaming ideas. Let's say that each day when you get up you say to yourself, "Instead of worrying about whether I am good enough, I want to know something else to do today." Then you look around and let one of the objects in the room "choose you." Of course the object is not really choosing you, you are the person who decides. But when you let yourself think of it that way and let it happen *as if you're being chosen,* your less-conscious, quieter mind can get in on the game and help you out. You can tell that you have been chosen when one of the following two things occurs:

a) an object sort of jumps out at you and says, "Me, me," (whether you really like that one or not);

b) an object keeps drawing your attention back to itself again and again—even when you look away at something else

The first object to choose you in one of these ways will be your teacher for the day.

How can a simple object teach you? Partly that depends on you. Say a little plant jumped out and said, "Me." To Pat, the meaning might be, "Bloom where you are planted today." To Ben, it might say, "Look at growing things around you today." To Marcella, it could mean, "God is here with you right now in this little plant." To Alain, it could mean, "Get outside where you can be yourself without thinking too much today." To Annie, it might say, "You did something good nurturing me." You can see that it is the inner self of each of these people that tells them what that plant means. Instead of letting their conscious, outside selves logically choose an item, they're letting their inner selves make an intuitive choice and tell them what that choice means to their unconscious.

Not very many people know how to allow their environment to support them in this way. But it's something everyone can learn.

Wouldn't it be nice to know you could get help every day just by listening to what your inner self says about the things around you?

Let's do the same thing with one more object, so that you can see that even "meaningless" objects can have meaning. Amy woke up today to an empty pop can beside her bed. For no reason she could think of, that pop can was what kept her attention. What might that mean? Well, depending on who Amy is it could mean:

- "Get rid of that old shame. Send it to recycling."
- "Call your pop today so you won't be ashamed of forgetting."
- "Even empty things have value. That includes you, Amy."
- "Eat something a little better for you today."
- "Clean up after yourself today and I won't be here remind you of what you didn't do."

Maybe you can think of still other things it would mean for you. But whatever was most right for her would be the mystery and the lesson for Amy today.

The Importance of a Sense of Purpose

One of the reasons that things like the preceding exercise can help with shame is that they give you a distinct sense of purpose, a simple guideline to follow. You also know that you're doing something constructive. When you allow yourself to notice how to heal, you're doing something very constructive for yourself. It's harder to call yourself names when you know you're already engaged in something to help yourself. It's not as easy to just agree with name-calling from others, either, when they try to shame you. You don't have to explain what you're doing if you believe they wouldn't understand. But no matter what they might say, you know that you're doing something active in your recovery from shame.

The World of Nature in Healing Shame

Another creative way to heal shame is to spend time in the world of nature. The creative spirit is everywhere there, from the inner-city tree full of nails that buds anyway, to the crow who follows you down the block when you imitate his cawing. The natural world is very helpful to the shamed spirit. Partly that's because most people don't feel so harshly examined or judged there. In many places, if you hold a handful of seeds up against a tree branch where there are chickadees, there is a good chance that, if you're patient, the chickadees will come and eat from your hand. Should they be shamed because they are trusting and vulnerable? Of course not—and neither should you. Your patience and openness to the chickadees, whether they eat from your hand or not, is something to be proud of. Most of nature accepts the windfalls and the tragedies that come through life with blaming or shaming. And in nature there is always growth, which is what you yourself are engaged in. Both you and the chickadees, or crows, or forest animals, or cows coming dubiously to the fence are curious. Curiosity is a form of hopefulness, and as you'll see in the next chapter, a wonderful antidote to shame.

So is getting out and walking, exploring your world. Being active can help a lot. Also, to be creative, you sometimes need to see creativity and growth. The natural world will give you an example and room to use your imagination in new ways, as well.

Exercises

1. Try something new. Choose one of the suggestions in the chapter above and try it out. Write your experience in your journal.

2. Make up a song about shame that would fit in your favorite kind of music. For example, something like, "The Low down Dirty-Shame Blues" (rhythm and blues), or "He Takes My Shame Away" (gospel), or "She Left Me on the Henhouse Floor the Day She Marched On out the Door. Ain't That a Shame" (country). Write the words down, make up a melody, and sing it to yourself the next time you get into a situation that would normally leave you feeling ashamed.

3. Go for a stroll. Notice the things that grab for your attention and go up close to them. Think about how they may be similar to you. Let yourself do this with several different objects or beings. Let yourself relax about doing this and don't work too hard.

Section II

Shame in Daily Life

Shame, Conformity, and Difference

Conformity Has Value

Conformity means that something is shaped to fit within certain standards. These are standards of common agreement among the group that uses them. For example, dollar bills are all very similar, and they're supposed to be. A vehicle without at least four rubber tires within a certain size range and its own working engine isn't likely to be considered a "car." This conformity means that when people talk about dollar bills or about cars, others know pretty much what they're referring to. Social standards are similar, though not always entirely the same in various groups of people. Although eating utensils may differ (silverware or chopsticks) and eating rules may vary (the manner of holding dinnerware in the U.S. versus the manner of holding dinnerware in Europe), the concept of "eating utensils" and "politeness" are both understood. Without common standards, people's general ability to communicate would be much more limited. Conformity is valuable because it can offer:

- an understanding of each other;
- more shared words and ideas for communication;
- a repertoire of common actions;
- a framework within which to define our own behavior;
- both general standards and ideals upon which to model our behavior.

Conforming to standards developed by the group to which you belong can provide you with the ability to determine whether you're behaving "correctly," and whether you have been acceptable to your group.

Conformity also helps people determine common moral codes—the prohibition against murder, for example. The force of conformity in a society helps to determine which social behaviors are considered exceptionally helpful or especially destructive. Conformity says, "This is a common pathway, tried before, and usually accepted and effective as a reasonable behavior."

The purposes of reasonable conformity are to:

- calm things down;
- create a set of fairly standard expectations people can follow;
- to establish some generally common values for a group or society;
- to teach through tradition and imitation.

Shame Enforces Conformity

Shame is the thing that tells people that they have left that path that has been established by social authority. When others are critical or shaming of their behavior, folks are compelled look to see how they have strayed from an important common standard or goal. When you shame yourself, you're saying to yourself that you recognize that you have strayed from the internal model you established for yourself. So, shame can let you know when you're not doing your best, and when you have violated common social codes that it would be better to keep intact.

Excessive Shame Can Enforce Excessive Conformity

Some people may need to learn the virtues of conformity. They may need help from others to attain a better balance between their own impulses and drives and the requirements of social living. Used wisely, the paths trod by others may provide very reliable and well-founded methods for living with less emotional pain.

However, those people who have been flooded by excessive shame are often those who understand the power of conformity best. These are also the people who may worry the most about their images in the world instead of identifying what they really need and want. Roberta was such a person. She grew up in a family that cared too much about how things looked to other people. Being "good" in her public behavior was drilled into her, and "How would that look?" was a regular comment in her family. Like most kids, she got teased and taunted by others in elementary school. That only got worse in junior high school, where what was "cool" seemed to change almost weekly, and where it seemed like nobody could really be secure. Then there was high school, and Roberta was not a charter member of the "in" group. When she was accepted—like when she helped on the yearbook—she felt like a phony, because she was often too anxious to really be herself. When she eventually came to talk about her shame, ten years later, she said several things that can help others understand the problems of conformity. Among them were:

> I was taught not to talk about family business outside my home. But even there, expressing my ideas seemed to provoke bad feelings. I would hear things from other family members like, "What about what my friends think?", "How could you even think of doing that to me?", "What will Grandma think if you wear that?", and "How would your dad look in the community if you did that? Don't you want to make us proud?"
>
> After a while I got into the habit of doing my best to look good, and if I didn't do what was expected of me, I'd hide it. But I was always worried. I would worry that maybe other people knew what I was thinking. I worried about the risk of getting caught doing the wrong thing—even when I hadn't done anything much at all. I felt like there was something wrong with me. Since I couldn't fix it, I just had to pretend I was normal.

By that point I had learned not to think too much. I tried to only think the way other people did and disregard things they didn't spend time thinking about. Most of the things I did were exactly the same as what my friends were doing. I acted pretty superficially. If my friends got away with it, I would try to be like them. But I never paid any attention to what I really liked or wanted. I just wanted to belong, without anybody really seeing me.

I'm still like that, and I admit I'm not having any fun. It's impossible to enjoy myself when I'm always worrying about what somebody else will think—whether I'm passing for normal or if people are making fun of me behind my back. But I can't tell anybody I know how I feel about this, either. I feel like I'm different from other people. They would just think I'm nuts.

Thanks to her to shame, Roberta has almost entirely exiled herself from the human community, while conforming more and more to how others behave. She had decided that there was something wrong with her and that she couldn't possibly be accepted the way she was, so she decided to simply imitate others. Shame has stopped Roberta from singing her own song as a human being. The need to conform has squelched any desire Roberta may have had to grow beyond the narrow boundaries she and society had determined for her.

Here are some examples of what people think when their motivations in life are shame-based, and they wish to be, to belong to, or to do something different from what they have been doing:

- What will other people think?

- Maybe they will think I am _____. (Fill in a negative term.)

- They will shame me (criticize me, laugh at me) for my choice.

- I'd better not try something new.

Although sometimes this decision-making process is appropriate, some people get so used to saying "No" to themselves that they radically shorten the process. They set very narrow standards for their possible behavior, and anything that even slightly stretches those standards gets ruled out immediately. In a sense, this is a lazy way out. They do not have to listen to themselves very carefully, nor do they have to make any moral decisions. They just don't do anything new.

Shame As a Weapon

Earlier we pointed out that shame can actually help protect the individual and help a person make better decisions. But shame and shaming inflicted by others can be a harsh master, oppressing individuals and groups as well. Shame can stop people from doing things that would dissolve reasonable social standards, but it can also be used as a weapon to reinforce unreasonable and unfair standards. One young man we know talked about growing up in a home where image and appearance were so important that he was not allowed to put his head back against the furniture without a towel. His parents were concerned that their children's hair might leave a spot or stain that a guest could see. Another woman shared how worried she had been as a child that she would be beaten if her behavior wasn't absolutely perfect when she was out with her parents. Another person remembered that he had been struck with the notion that his family often seemed to be lying to everyone else in order to pretend that the family was "a good family." In all these cases, the children learned that what things look like is much more important than how things really are or how people might feel. They were taught that *image* is more significant than reality. When people learn that the way they look is more important than the way they feel, shame is the result. Shame results because the emphasis on image says, "Your inside cannot meet the standards that your outside must meet." Therefore, someone given the message unavoidably thinks that there is something wrong with them, and they feel defective.

This kind of shaming can make an individual very reluctant to be even a little different from their neighbor. It dampens a person's excitement. It can stop exploration. It can be used to enforce completely unreasonable standards as well as reasonable ones. At its worst, it can set individuality off limits, so that a person not adhering to the decisions of a community group can be shunned and driven not only from their community but also from their family. Shame can be used by a group to limit its members to only those who are alike by defining such differences as in skin color, weight, gender, or lifestyle as wholly bad. Shame can be used to create and enforce the worst kinds of prejudice and/or mindless conformity even on the part of those who only want to be good people and do things right.

If shame were as devastating as people fear it will be, though, the world would be less various than it is. Conformity would have become the rule across groups that still have many differences. Big changes could not take place in such a short time as a generation. We change too much for shame and the conformity it is used to enforce to be the rule. What is it that combats the shame?

Difference Balances Shame

The fact is that conformity and difference exist in a kind of balance. Each is essential. Each has its own value to give to the world. For the individual, conformity provides steadiness and predictability. It supports the act of learning through the imitation of others who have already mastered something. It suggests that learning by tradition will be very helpful, and that a common value system underlies common behaviors. For the group, conformity provides a regularity of habits that are beneficial to the group and a way for members of the group to communicate about these habits. It increases the ability of a group to establish rules for internal cooperation and to cooperate with other groups without losing their own group identity. And it enables the formation of society-wide values and goals that are meaningful.

Conformity only becomes a problem when people are too intimidated or shamed to continue learning. When that happens, those people lose the excitement of exploring their own talents. Shame can be used by a family, a group, a community, or a society to rigidly suppress variation, alternate visions, or the participation of a particular group in the social good. Then conformity becomes a threat to the survival and the thriving of either that particular group or society as a whole. It's as if the head and heart had decided that because the liver processes poison, it will no longer be allowed to have any significant part in how the body is run. The arrogance of the head and heart in this situation will eventually destroy the body—and sooner or later, the liver must be acknowledged.

Difference is an essential part of a necessary balance. Without the liver, the head could not work clearly and the heart would accumulate toxic levels of poison. In terms of people operating within a group, difference provides a legitimate place for creative thinking. It increases the survival ability of an individual person by encouraging innovative uses for what that person has and by stimulating experimentation and exploration of new tools for thought and action. Difference allows a person to grow by choosing directions that may seem tangential to others, and encourages curiosity, excitement, challenge, and daring. Difference is a deeper process than simply reacting to and rejecting what others are doing. It is an act of its own that moves a person further in their own development in life. It is true that in isolation an individual or a group may develop a constellation of differences that both define and make communication with other groups more difficult, but that is not inherent in the concept of difference.

Socially, difference increases options for living for everyone and multiplies the ways that people can choose to achieve what is most important to them. Difference tells people that flexibility can help them survive better and achieve more. Flexibility and variation increase the group's possibilities for success by allowing the exploration and discovery of good options by many various members of the group. Difference can teach groups and the individuals within those groups to learn success strategies both from others within their own group, and from other groups, as well.

So, difference and conformity both contribute quite a bit to the survival and the thriving of individual human beings, families, communities, and societies. Changes can and do take place fairly quickly in the scheme of things when they are necessary. Some force must be at work in the human psyche to encourage so very much difference in cultures, worship, talents, and behaviors.

There must be something powerful opposing shame because evolution itself is based partly on experimentation and difference. It is the mutations of the usual that survive and become the rule in future generations. But for that to occur, chance, risks, and failures must be quite commonplace. Clearly, human beings have many similarities to each other. And equally clear is the fact that human beings are not exactly the same. And since there are quite a few areas in human experience where differences are tolerated and even encouraged, there must be a pretty strong force opposing the shame that would keep differences under wraps.

So, if shame stimulates more conformity, then what stimulates more difference? If shame helps to create and enforce security, what is strong enough to balance that? With all of the forces for conformity in this world, what is it that balances people so that they can allow, desire, and even encourage difference?

Curiosity and Difference

The answer to the question about what promotes difference is one every child knows from the start. It is *curiosity*. In the human psyche, inside every person, curiosity acts as the "opposite" of shame. Shame ensures that excitement doesn't cause you to reach too far all at once. Curiosity is the balance that stimulates a person's excitement to uncover the new and different. Curiosity is a force different from pride but just as important in opposing shame.

Many human beings have mixed feelings about curiosity. There is something in people that likes similarity and they often fear the uncertainty of change. In many ways people *do* like dressing similarly to others, knowing in advance how to behave, and knowing what they're supposed to be doing. Human beings are reassured by the norms and standards that are reinforced by shame. In many respects, people just want to keep the world circumscribed within clearly identifiable boundaries. That conservatism is why cultures have such adages as, "Curiosity killed the cat," and "A bird in the hand is worth two in the bush." "Be cautious," these adages seem to say. "Don't get too excited. Don't get carried away. Pandora just gave the world problems, because she had to know what was in that box. Don't you be like that." Because people have such mixed feelings, they reinforce shame with fear, hoping to build a double defense against the flame of curiosity.

But in truth, human beings are attracted to what is different. What's different captures their attention, even if it's something quite simple. Difference stirs people up a bit. It gets them going. "A hot dog on a stick? What're you gonna use for a bun? Inside corn bread on the stick, and it comes like that? That I gotta see. Let's go down there." "What is *that*?" people say, and get up closer to inspect the whatchamacallit. Pretty soon there's a crowd. "What's up?" they say wanting to know the "news." "What's happening?" "How did they do that?" "Who would even dream of that?" "Oh gosh, come and look at this!" Difference excites human curiosity, and people behave just like Pandora or that cat . . . except that people don't always exercise a cat's native cautiousness.

Then the same people turn right around and tell their partners that there is only one good or customary way to do the dishes, get the wash done, hang a picture, or change the oil. And just for "oomph," they call that way "the right way," so that shame will back them up. When it comes to something that they've made into a habit, they will often try both to convince and to shame another person into doing it the same way, because that reassures them that their way *is* right.

The truth is that there are many good ways to wash the dishes or perform various tasks, and others will usually come up with great alternatives if they're not shamed for being curious. That's true for you, too. If you have been excessively shamed or if you have ever embarrassed yourself because you were curious, then your curiosity may have become an area of shame for you.

If you're ashamed to be different from everyone else, you'll feel compelled to shame yourself when you are curious. "Don't even think about it," or "Don't get ideas in your head," you might say to yourself. What you would mean is, "Don't get excited and don't be too curious." And when you remain curious, you would tell yourself that there is something wrong with you. But that is simply not true. People's excitement and curiosity will speak up often, if they are willing to listen to them, and these emotions are the balance for shame in people's lives. Yes, people can be led "too far down the garden path." For example, one lady in her late fifties got so excited about finding alternate ways to wash the dishes that she invented an entire kitchen that washed the dishes and all of its surfaces as well, including the floor. You would have to leave the room if you didn't want to get washed down, too. But the system worked quite well and resulted in very clean dishes. However, this system would probably be too different for most of us. Instead of being regarded as a pioneer, the woman who invented the system was consigned to the oblivion of an "eccentric," those we think are a few pickles short of a full barrel. This is a good example of taking one's curiosity a little further than others can readily understand. However, she still took pride in her creation. It did what she hoped it would do. It was a wonderful experiment that must have taught her many practical things in its creation. She may be considered a little eccentric, may be thought to have gone too far, but the term "going too far" with curiosity is hard to define. Even if you take this lady as a model of the extreme, you can probably see that you can experiment and explore much more than you might normally and still stay within normal parameters.

Curiosity Exposes What Is Hidden

Often people have learned to be ashamed of things in themselves that they could take pride in. You may feel ugly or ashamed of looks quite unnecessarily. You may be ashamed of your income but still contribute to charity because it's the right thing to do. You may believe you play an instrument poorly, but provide happiness to your friends each time you play. You may feel as if you shouldn't take up so much space, when in fact other people are always happy to see you coming because they experience you as kind, or smart, or helpful, or good company. If you stay hidden in your shame, of course, you'll never find these things out. But there is nothing shameful at all about asking others how they think or feel about you. Usually this is regarded as an act of trust. You must, in fact, trust yourself enough to ask others what they really see in you, to help you appreciate it in yourself.

Being curious about yourself is the opposite of cutting yourself off from self-interest. If people learn to "Do as others do," "Follow the leader," "Take care of others because they are more important," or to "Just don't even think about it," they effectively cut themselves off from aspects of themselves that can help them the most in the healing of their shame. If you have cut yourself off from other people who don't seem like you because you're afraid of difference, you have alienated an important part of yourself. In both cases, you have shamed yourself out of exploring. It is true, certain kinds of exploring can lead to unconsidered consequences. But you don't have to try *everything* in order to nurture your curiosity and excitement and find out about yourself. All you have to do is to question what others have already told you about yourself and see if, in fact, it's true.

Mary was told she was impractical, manipulative, greedy, and malicious. As long as she believed this, she stayed away from finding out who she was. She conformed and followed all the rules she could find because she didn't want others to discover that she was really a bad person. When challenged to do some research on how she has behaved in the past and how she acts now, Mary discovered:

- in a lot of ways, she was and still is impractical, but if she wants she can change some of this;

- she isn't very manipulative at all, unless she is afraid. If she is fearful and doesn't stay thoughtful, she can manipulate by avoiding others, but she has a long history of refusing to use others for her own purposes;

- she does have an eating disorder and at times overeats. This seems to be mostly to comfort herself, and even so, she has no trouble sharing bites or portions or goodies with others. She tends to buy more things for others than she does for herself. She really doesn't seem very greedy, although she does occasionally feel somewhat needy of support from others;

- she does many things to avoid hurting others, although when asked for her opinion, she is honest. She has worked hard on forgiveness in her life, and no longer experiences revengeful feelings when something goes wrong. She cannot remember trying to hurt anyone on purpose in the last ten years.

After Mary looked at herself carefully, she discovered that she felt much better about herself than she had thought she would. She had been afraid to be curious about herself because of her beliefs that she was what she had been called. Now she realizes that she is the only person who really knows what goes on inside her and therefore, she is the expert on who she is. She experiences more pride on a daily basis, checks in with herself both physically and emotionally, and has engaged in some new activities since she realizes that she could be having a lot more fun than she was allowing herself. Mary's curiosity about herself has been very healing for her.

Being curious about others can give you a lot of information you couldn't have had before, and help to alter your view of yourself as well. If you've been continuously criticized or shamed by others, you may have come to believe what they say about you. If you regularly pick up tension from others, and you tend to be shame-based, you may assume that any tension is about you. Information about others can help you get to the truth in the situation.

Kim grew up in a family setting where she was not a birth child, and where she was the most criticized of the children in the home. Married to Martin, she felt really incompetent. She never seemed to be able to do anything right, even when she tried her hardest. She decided she must be dumb, because she couldn't seem to learn how to do things right. When she began to have children, she read a lot and took classes in child care so her children would be able to count on her. She was not surprised that Martin criticized her care of the children. She thought that he was probably right. However, as the kids became toddlers and preschoolers, she began to chafe at how he criticized them.

He seemed to think that they couldn't do anything right. But the books and classes had taught her that Martin was not being reasonable with them, and that the way he was handling situations with the children would not teach the children much that was positive. It wouldn't even really help them please Martin. At a counselor's suggestion, Kim began to ask herself if Martin was being reasonable with her. She even did some experiments to discover the truth. She discovered that, no matter how she did some things, he would criticize them, even if she had done them exactly the way he asked her to do them. She hadn't noticed that before. She also noticed that he was more critical in certain situations and at certain times than others. This gave her the information that he was depending on prescription medication too much, and that "things going wrong" seemed to be a signal to criticize her and then take another pill. These observations helped her to understand that: 1) part of the problem was not her problem at all—it had to do with Martin and his overuse of medicine; 2) that Martin needed to learn how to parent the children just as much as she had needed to, and that he certainly was not an expert in that department. Therefore, she would have to stand up for the children at times rather than letting Martin be constantly critical of them; and 3) that Martin seemed to use criticizing others in order to feel better about himself. That might mean that when he called her dumb, it was to make himself feel smart, not because she really was dumb.

Kim began to stand up for herself and the children, and when they went to school, she went back to school too. She feels much better about herself today, and has confronted Martin about his problems. It feels good to her to know how to separate her emotional "stuff" from his. Mentally, she pictures an "in-box" that says "hers" and a trash can that says "his." If he says something she thinks she should consider, it goes in the in-box. If she knows that he is just being critical and shaming because he's not feeling good about himself, it goes in the trash can. When she gets time, she sorts through the things in her mental in-box, then mentally gives the trash can to Martin to empty, taking it back ready for the next critical remark. She doesn't worry about it anymore.

Bob felt tense every time he was around his boss. He figured the tension was his, that he just didn't know how to behave to defuse it. He figured he should be able to change the feelings of tension, and that he must be doing something wrong. He began to cross-examine himself on everything he did and was almost ready to quit his job, when he finally asked his boss if he was doing something wrong. His boss told him he was the best worker he had ever had in that business, and he was really happy with him. Bob didn't have to quit, but he did feel the need to then say that he thought there had been a lot of tension in the air. His boss said that that was true, but it wasn't about Bob. He was going through some problems at home with his son that worried him deeply and he had trouble putting it out of his mind at work. In fact, Bob's boss went so far as to admit that he wished he could count on his son to accept him in the way he felt Bob did.

Checking out what was going on helped Bob keep his job, and gain an appreciation for his boss's humanity. He quit projecting and assuming that everything must be about him. In fact, in a couple of months things got better between the boss and his son, and it was a lot more fun to work there. Bob went on to take over the business when his boss retired. He had learned one thing, though, that he did better than his boss. He told new workers how they were doing right up front, so they didn't have to wonder.

In all three of these situations, the pursuit of curiosity helped to heal shame, sometimes very long-standing shame. Shame is a secretive state, and the excitement and joy of acting on one's curiosity is often helpful in the important task of exposing shame in a safe way. Only Bob felt safe enough to talk to his boss about the problem. Mary and Kim both talked to others who were safe, and did not necessarily have to confide in the people who were helping to create their shame. Either route can be a good place to start.

Curiosity Helps Heal Division

Curiosity is a genuine wish to know or understand something. Most people are flattered when someone else takes such an interest in them. It often means that the other person wants to learn about them. But, if someone is a member of a minority group, the curiosity of others who don't belong to the same group can trigger their shame in the sense that they may feel set apart and different again. Reciprocal curiosity can do a lot toward establishing a peer relationship. If a person somehow hasn't accepted that wider sense of defectiveness, they might not have to go through that rush of shame. But the fact is that shame can be and is used by society to enforce prejudice against certain groups. Uninformed biases do affect everyone in minority groups. We encourage everyone to use their curiosity to cross some of the false boundaries established by shame, and to get to know many other people as individuals. When you behave as genuine learners and teachers for yourself and others, you can learn a great deal about the world and about yourself. Human curiosity has a power to do away with the stigma of shame for everyone. Oppressed or oppressors, the same and different, everyone is in this together. The better people know each other, the better they can work together.

Curiosity Can Overcome Both Shame and Difference

Imagine two religious services in the same church, temple, or mosque. In one case, the leader of the service is formal and very serious. All members are quiet, mostly unmoving, listening closely to the leader. In the other service the leader, while serious, expresses more feeling. The members of the service whisper, comment to each other, and even shout back at the leader. They move around a lot, wiggling in their chairs, jumping up, and moving their arms. If you were a regular member of one, the other might dismay you. You might judge and say, "These folks don't know how to behave." You might say, "These folks act like they're dead. They've got no joy. What're they here for?" Of course, in either case, curiosity could give you an answer. Notice that these groups of people worshipping are not connected to different religious or cultural groups. They are simply practicing two significantly different ways of worshipping: One is the service where the leader is seen as a wise teacher and model to be listened to quietly and deferentially. The other service is a participatory service, where people are encouraged to gather around verbally and sometimes physically to participate in worshipping as an organic group. Wouldn't it be wonderful if anyone could do both of these without those judgments?

Conformity is useful, helping people communicate and achieve common goals. Shame can help remind you when you abandon the agreed-upon goals and values of your self and your community. But shame can also become a weapon used to enforce too much conformity. Shame can be used to criticize and condemn differences that are neutral and harmless or even quite positive.

When things that are the same are seen as better than things that are different, many people tend to overconform, losing track of the special skills, creative ways of looking, or playful perspectives they carry within. You may begin to feel that your uniqueness is worthless, irrelevant, silly, or crazy. When individuality is overrun by conformity, the whole community loses vitality.

Luckily, there is an antidote to having too much shame inhibiting, and it's built right into human beings. Even the most thorough conformist can get curious about differences—what they are, what they are based in, and what they accomplish. Curiosity is also one of the best ways to get to know yourself when you have gathered too many shame experiences. It can help to balance you.

One way to see this is to imagine a tightrope walker going across a rope of community expectations. To get across, the tightrope walker needs a balance pole that he himself can use directly. That balance pole allows him to make the side-to-side movements that go with walking, so he can actually get somewhere. You, the person, walk daily on the rope of community values, expectations, and agreed-upon ways of life. If you do not use the balance pole of curiosity and difference in your own way at each step, you may fall, or you may stand in one spot, paralyzed and afraid to move. But with your balance pole and your own ability to adjust it to meet your own needs, you can walk across that rope with a sense of mastery.

Exercises

1. How do you worry about what others will think? Think about that for a minute. Divide it into two questions:
   a) **When** do you worry most about what people will think? (For example, when company's coming, when you meet someone, at work.)
   b) **What** do you fear they will think of you? (Give examples of what you would worry about them thinking in three or more situations.)

   Now, giving it some careful thought, how many of these negative attitudes about you are actually your own opinions, coming from your own background or your own critical feelings about yourself? When you shame yourself about situations in category "a," what names do you call yourself? What is the worst thing that would happen if someone thought these things of you? Why do you think these things about yourself?
   Be curious, and write the answers in your journal.

2. People say, "Curiosity killed the cat." But they also say, "Cats have nine lives."
   Make a list of three or four things that you would love to do or explore but feel you can't because others might see you as "crazy," "dumb," or "out of it." Examples: volunteer for the Seti project watching for alien communications; taking up the accordion (or fife, guitar, or flute), no matter how old you are; joining an organization you've secretly wanted to belong to; painting a rainbow on your front door. Put things you really would love to do on your list and then choose one to actually do. Notice your excitement and your curiosity as you open up to another part of yourself. Practice the cautious curiosity of a cat.

3. Let yourself notice reactions in yourself or in others that you really might not be understanding. Instead of immediately criticizing either yourself or them, ask questions about what is going on. Notice that mystery is a part of life, but that there are many things that do not need to remain a mystery and that there are many things you do not need to explain.

Body Shame and Sexual Shame

My Body—Friend or Foe?

The exercise seemed simple enough when we assigned it to our group of adult students, teachers, ministers, and nurses. "Write down ten things you appreciate about your stomach." So why the groans and gallows humor? The attempts to delay? The reluctance to talk? The answer soon became obvious. People were struggling to come up with even one or two positive things to say about their stomachs. It would have been so much easier, they said, if only we'd asked them to write ten things they *disliked*. Then they could talk about how their stomachs were flabby and greedy and ugly and bad.

If there is one area in American society most connected with excessive shame that area is surely how Americans relate to their bodies. For every American man or woman who feels a calm acceptance of their body there are certainly many more who continually reject, neglect, or obsess over their bodies, all the while feeling inadequate because of what they see as their bodily defects.

Let's begin this chapter with messages consistent with bodily pride. If you are friends with your own body, you'll have thoughts like these: My body is good; it's good enough; I like my body; I belong in this body; my body is competent (I can do what I need to do with my body); my body is an important part of me; I want to care for my body; I take pride in my body. You'll act on those thoughts as well, treating your body with respect by eating well, exercising appropriately, and so on. You won't, however, obsess about your body, constantly trying to perfect it. Basically, you will "own" your body, accepting it as a natural and important part of your being.

Even people with pride about their bodies sometimes feel bodily shame. But their shame stays within normal limits, which means it's temporary, moderate, and leads toward improved behavior. Basically, they'll feel shame about temporary bodily failings that they can correct or accept. Some of these failures may be relatively trivial such as finding a dirt smudge on your nose just when you thought you looked really good. They may also feel shame about more significant bodily failures such as a bout of sexual impotence or a serious illness that suddenly limits what they can do. But in all these cases they aren't crushed by their shame. Instead, they correct what they can and accept the rest. As they age, for instance, people with bodily pride learn to work within the boundaries of their diminishing capacities without hating themselves for something they cannot control.

The Origins of Body Shame

Shame is a very physical experience. You may blush and stammer, look away and shrink down. You could feel totally exposed and become paralyzed while at the same time wanting to run. No wonder, then, that people associate shame with their bodies. The more that people have been shamed, especially in childhood, the more likely they will carry their shame in and on their bodies, perhaps developing a permanent slouch or totally blank stare. Indeed, body shame can become a shorthand signal of a deeper self shame. Certainly many authors (one writer is Roth, 1991) who write on the topic of eating disorders, note that shame about bodily appearance often covers up a deeper shame about the self. That doesn't mean that you should ignore body shame and just treat it as a cover for self-shame, though. Once body shame takes root in one's being it definitely needs to be treated as a distinct and important problem.

American society is tremendously shaming about the body. Just watching a few hours of television exposes people to innumerable advertisements urging people to eradicate all traces of human odors, fat, baldness, incontinence, impotence, and any other imperfection. Of course they are also urged toward excess at the same time, to eat and drink everything in sight. It's impossible to do all that at the same time. The result is that people are set up to feel shame no matter what they do or don't do with their bodies. Worse yet, they are trained to treat their bodies as objects, as things to be manipulated. But it is inherently shame producing to treat any person as an object, including your own self. People become shame bound when they treat their bodies as if they were things that need to be controlled instead of truly acceptable parts of themselves.

And then there is the American insistence on comparison making, especially among women. Whose body is prettier? Handsomer? Sexier? Americans compare bodies endlessly, triggering perpetual bouts of envy and shame. Nobody really wins these battles. We've had beautiful women in therapy who hate their bodies even though they're supposedly winning the admiration battle. Shame isn't really about winning or losing these comparisons, after all. It's about not being able to accept your body as good enough just as it is.

Another source of shame is American society's basic ambivalence toward the functions of the human body, especially sexuality. This ambivalence extends to a simultaneous obsession and repression with regard to sexuality. The average citizen is exposed to thousands of titillating scenes that hover on the edge of shamelessness—in advertisements, magazine stories, books, and films. However, people are still expected to act with discretion and modesty. Somehow they must be excited and unexcited simultaneously, both turned on and turned off. Men and women both are expected simultaneously to be virgins and whores, innocent and knowledgeable, pure and lustful. How could bodily and sexual shame not develop in this hothouse atmosphere? How can people accept their bodies when they must simultaneously renounce and indulge them?

Women are especially vulnerable to body and sexual shame because of societal confusion about their visibility. Should women look and act enticingly? The answer right now is that women are expected to present an image of sexual availability without really being available. It's as if women are told that they must dress in a bikini but must also always look down. Body shame and doubt are more likely to develop when people can't distinguish modest from immodest, private from public, and open from secretive behavior. This ambivalent attitude produces doubt as well as shame about bodies. "Will I ever be good enough?" is a question many people ask about their bodies and their sexual behavior. Somehow people are expected to gain the knowledge and skills to be experts in bed. Otherwise they fear they'll disappoint their partners, risking rejection. But at the same time they can't be *too* good lest they risk getting labeled as shameless, "dirty," or sinful.

Finally, we've seen that excessively puritanical religious training can be a source of body and sexual shame. Christianity, in particular, with its central theme of the virgin birth, has traditionally had difficulty separating shame from the body. The resulting mixed message: "Go out and multiply . . . but don't have any fun doing it," is a poor compromise that leaves many people confused about reconciling their spiritual faith with their lustful and sinful bodies.

Somehow each person must find their own path through this particular shame wilderness. The goal is to disregard the constant barrage of mixed messages and find a way to accept your body as your own.

Three Patterns of Body Shame

Excessive body shame is likely to show up in three ways: disownership of your body; obsession with your body; disgust with your body. Objectification of the self occurs in all three situations but how people deal with their body is different in each.

You can tell that *disownership* of the body has occurred when a person seems to have lost interest in their body. Neglect is common in this situation. Body disowners simply don't take enough interest in their bodies for scheduled maintenance like dental care and physical checkups. Good clothing is a waste of time. So is exercise and proactive physical care. Sexuality, too, may be neglected or ignored. It's not that these people consciously hate their bodies. Rather, they've resolved their body-shame issues by attempting to ignore their bodies. The underlying rationale is this: "If I don't think about or attend to my body then I don't have to feel ashamed of it." This way of handling body shame certainly does minimize your immediate shame and pain. But it cannot lead to body pride or acceptance.

Obsession with your body is another sign of body shame. In this case people try to grow perfect bodies but usually end up focusing upon all their alleged defects—those extra ten pounds, the too-long nose, those flabby quadriceps. This excessive self-involvement hints broadly of shame. And, like all perfectionistic solutions to the shame dilemma, this kind of obsession inevitably leads to failure. Eventually the body collapses under the weight of unreasonable demand. Each collapse triggers waves of shame that only lead to renewed attempts to eradicate body shame through even greater effort.

Disgust with one's body is yet another evidence of body shame. Here people turn away from their own bodies, as if there was something horribly wrong with them. They take in everybody's criticism of their bodies and add a lot more of their own creation. The result is an overwhelming belief that their bodies are thoroughly repulsive: "Ugh, I hate my body. It stinks. It's ugly. I would never want to be with someone who looks like me." These people aren't hiding their body shame from themselves or others. Instead, they're promoting it for everyone to see. Perhaps in that manner they at least wrest a sense of control away from their shame. It's a little better that they can control how and when they humiliate themselves rather than let others attack them without warning. But this kind of body shame exacts a tremendous price. It makes people believe that their bodies can only be now and forever a source of shame.

Any person may experience one, two, or all three of these ways of rejecting their bodies. Fortunately, excessive body shame can be challenged, as we will describe later in this chapter.

Sexual Shame

The three signs of bodily shame just mentioned—neglect, obsession, and disgust—apply equally in the area of sexuality. Some people habitually disown and neglect their sexual impulses, treating them as unimportant or irrelevant. These individuals frequently grew up in homes where every hint of sexuality was eradicated. The parents in these families usually did not touch or hold each other, much less kiss, pet, or talk about sexuality. The message they may have wanted to convey was that sexuality is good but a private matter. But that's not what some of their children concluded. Instead these kids decided that sexuality was shameful, a drive that must be rejected in their lives. They then ignore and neglect their sexuality, starving it in the hope that it will die forever. This may work to a certain extent, at least at a conscious level. But, for most people, their sexuality doesn't go away so much as go underground, temporarily suppressed but ready to be reclaimed.

Sexual obsession is the flip side of disownership. Here people dwell on their sexual appearance and performance. Indeed, the very word "performance" epitomizes the concept of sexual obsession. What is a performance but something you watch, try to perfect, but never quite experience completely? Sexual performers objectify both their own and their partner's bodies. Sex then becomes something you do *to* rather than *with* another.

Sexual addiction is an extreme form of shame-based sexual obsession and compulsion. Sexual addicts may spend hours every day purchasing and trading pornographic materials, masturbating, displaying their bodies, attempting another conquest, or engaging in sexual encounters. The sexual addict's sexual shame has been transformed into apparent shamelessness. "Look at me, go ahead look. I have no sexual shame," is the message of the sexual addict. But usually their bravado masks tremendous shame about their bodies, their sexuality, and their inability to develop emotionally intimate relationships.

Many people with excessive shame turn away with disgust from their sexuality. Too often (but not always) these individuals were the victims of incest or other forms of sexual abuse when children. They may have come to hate their bodies because they believe that is what attracted unwanted advances. Besides, they correctly felt sexually used by someone who should have protected them. Their bodies became objects. It's easy to become ashamed and disgusted with the entire idea of sexuality when it becomes linked with disrespectful treatment (whether as children or adults).

Others with sexual disgust may come from rigidly religious or moralistic families that shamed every hint of sexuality. In doing so, these families turned sexuality into something forbidden and dangerous, something that happened to you rather than being a natural part of you. Children raised in these families often struggle against feelings that every sexual encounter, even with those they love, is dirty and shameful. They are particularly repulsed when their bodies demand sexual gratification despite the opposition of their minds or morals. Then they feel out of control, held in the grasp of their lower, shameful passions.

Sexual shame and disgust may develop if people are told as children or adults that they are ugly, fat, unattractive. "You are disgusting. Your body is repulsive. Nobody would ever want you," is what these people hear over and over. It's hard not to believe those messages. After a while people accept them and condemn their own bodies.

Another group who become sexually disgusted reside in loveless marriages that they haven't the courage to leave. These are the clients who come to therapy, even couples counseling, complaining that they simply can't stand to share a bed with their partner any longer. They often feel that their bodies are being used by their partners for selfish gratification. They may even think of themselves as little better than prostitutes, trading sexual favors for financial or family security. Eventually they find just about everything their partner says or does repulsive, sexually or otherwise. But really they are reacting to the shame they feel for staying stuck in an unfulfilling relationship. Their sexual revulsion is more a signal of their deeper shame than a permanent part of their being. Probably their sexual disgust would disappear if they loved and felt loved by their partner.

The Shame/Sexuality/Intimacy Connection

Sexual contact is a passionate but not inherently dignified act. The idea, after all, is to lose control, at least temporarily, and nothing demands immediate loss of control more than the overwhelming feelings during orgasm. Naked, impelled by powerful need, physically intertwined, and emotionally enmeshed, it's obvious that the possibility of shame and humiliation always hovers around the most passionate embrace. No wonder some individuals prefer to avoid sexuality as much as possible while others turn away from their own desires because of their shame.

Still, most sexual encounters are not shaming. That's because most participants choose to respect each other and themselves. Instead of shaming the other person ("Is that as hard as you get?"; "Why does it take you so long to come?") most people try to practice tact, modesty, and discretion. Positive, moderate shame helps make this mutually respectful interaction happen.

We've mentioned previously that there is such a thing as good, normal shame. Nowhere is this more true than in the area of sexuality. In fact, real intimacy might not be possible without shame (Schneider 1977). That's because positive shame throws a protective barrier around sexuality, turning it into a private event rather than a public spectacle.

Normal shame has two main uses in the sexual arena. First, it slows down and socializes sexuality. When necessary, normal shame sends messages that this is not the time nor the place nor the right person with which to be sexual. Because sexuality is a difficult drive to control, these messages are not always successful. However, they work well enough to make monogamy possible. A limited amount of shame encourages people to find appropriate outlets for their sexual drive without destroying it.

The second major use of sexual shame is to help people develop a capacity for emotional intimacy. Here's an illustration. Think of a couple of teenagers caught up in the throes of passion. Temporarily blind to anything but their desire, they fondle and do even more wherever they happen to be. This behavior creates a field of embarrassment for everybody else in the vicinity. People watch furtively, turn away, and then peek again. Shame shimmers around the space. Yes, the sexuality on display excites but it also feels wrong. Teens or not, they need to take their passion somewhere private. Only then might their lust have a chance to become love.

Sexuality is wonderful partly because it feels great all by itself. But sexual desire also promotes emotional intimacy, the sense that you can trust another with your secrets and feelings, as well as your body. This doesn't happen automatically, though. Intimacy only thrives where there is privacy. After all, the idea of intimacy itself implies sharing parts of your identity with someone special, hopefully someone who will honor your disclosures with the bond of secrecy. So shame, if not excessive, helps people discover that sexual freedom with another can lead to emotional freedom, sexual respect to emotional respect, and sexual intimacy to emotional intimacy. Intimacy develops as each partner learns that he or she will treat the other with honor even though they could shame them.

Mutually respectful sexual experiences help people develop positive sexual identities. Those with this identity feel sexually competent without having to perform. They experience their humanity, their intrinsic connection with others, in their sexuality. They act upon their sexual impulses with discretion, building the possibility for emotional intimacy into their sexual experiences. Most of their sexual encounters are pleasant celebrations of the life force that resides within us all. They can and do discuss their sexuality with their partners, although almost always (because of the link between sexuality and privacy) with a little embarrassment or discomfort. They neither flaunt their sexuality through rampant exhibitionism nor try to hide all signs of it through excessive prudishness. Their sexuality is simply part of their goodness.

Homosexuality: Stigmatized Sexuality

Homosexuality, despite the evidence that it may be gathering gradual acceptance in American society, remains a sexual preference that is often accompanied by shame. Certainly not all homosexuals are ashamed of themselves. However, many gay men and lesbian women, especially those not living in large urban centers, must keep their identities secret to avoid harassment, discrimination, and physical threat.

Stigma is a term that refers to how entire groups of people can be shamed just because of their group membership. Groups may be stigmatized on the basis of race, gender, religion, language, and certainly sexuality. To be stigmatized means that people tend to think of members of these groups first as "that kind of person" and secondly, if at all, as a human being. Joseph, the human who happens to be gay, becomes Joseph, the homosexual who may or may not be considered human.

Social stigma takes shame from the individual to the societal plane. In a sense it is more American society as a whole that has a shame problem with homosexuality than any particular person. This suggests that homosexual people cannot fully avoid the issue of shame even if they feel perfectly comfortable and proud of their gay identity. For example, imagine how much attention two men walking down the street holding hands will receive in many communities. "Look," people will say, "two gay men," when they would never think to point out a heterosexual couple. This excessive curiosity, even if apparently free from judgment, still is shaming in that relatively private behavior is given public scrutiny.

Almost every homosexual man or woman must struggle sooner or later with the issues of shame and pride: "Why won't people just accept me for who I am, regardless of my sexuality?" "Will I tell my parents this year, or ever, about my partner?" "Can I really accept myself as a gay person?" These are difficult questions made even harder because of the shame attached by society to homosexuality.

One important note: Just because someone is gay doesn't mean that all their shame concerns relate to that reality. Shame and pride come from many sources.

Reclaiming Your Body and Sexuality

The critical problem here is that somehow shame has become fused with your body or your sexuality. Your body and sexuality have become shame bound. The goal, then, is first to break the linkage between shame and this aspect of your being and then to promote the development of healthy pride about your body and sexuality. You must, in essence, reclaim your right to your body and sexuality and thus free yourself from shame's dictatorial powers. This reclamation project will take time, of course. You'll need to be patient with yourself as you proceed. But you can be optimistic as well. Body shame and sexuality shame do heal. It's very possible to reclaim full use and acceptance of your body and sexuality.

In general, the things that work with all kinds of shame are also important in this area. You'll need to think about how shame is affecting you right now, specific shame experiences relating to your body and sexual history, shameful messages about your body and sexuality as well as the source and origin of these messages, and how you might challenge these beliefs and substitute new ideas about your body and sexuality that will help you feel better about yourself. You'll also need to ask yourself how much these particular shame issues mask a deeper shame about your entire self. Sometimes body shame and sexual shame distract from this more global problem with self-evaluation. If so you'll need to deal both with your body and sexual shame and the deeper shame about yourself rather than just one or the other.

What would you want to do with your body if you could reclaim it? What would you do with your sexual being?

Now let's deal with ways to help undo excessive body and sexual shame in the three specific areas noted previously in this chapter: disownership and neglect; obsession; and disgust.

Disownership and Neglect

Body disowners have to give themselves permission to have and use their bodies. That means breaking the rule that says it's shameful to have a body. But that's exactly the rule that has held disowners captive. That rule must be challenged. Body disowners need to find a substitute belief that feels right to them. Your statement might be, "I choose to reclaim my body and my sexuality." Or, if that seems too strong, perhaps, "I won't treat my body as an enemy anymore," or "I'm willing to start noticing my body more than I used to."

After choosing your body-acceptance statement, you'll want to take action to implement your new belief. The key is to realize that paying attention is the opposite of neglect. Attending to your body and sexuality is exactly what the neglecter must do to break the shame/body fusion. You've got to let yourself get curious and interested in your body and sexuality. Above all, you'll need to attend to what your body wants and needs: touching, holding, caressing, stroking, and so on, in sexual and nonsexual forms. You might need more information about how your body works as well. You can get that knowledge by journaling, reading on the body and sexuality, walking, exercising, and dancing. Basically you'll be seeking answers to some fundamental questions: what do I feel, what do I want and need, what does my body want to do, and what are my desires?

Obsession

Healing body and sexual obsession centers around the phrase "good enough." My body is good enough. My sexuality is good enough. I am good enough. This contrasts with the fear "I'll never be good enough," that's at the root of obsession. Only by accepting your body and your sexuality as you are can you break the desperate needs to perfect your body and perform in bed.

If at all possible, it's time to minimize comparing your body with everybody else's. Remember that American society is fiercely competitive at the body level. But too much competition leads only to shame and failure. No matter how hard you try, someone else will inevitably come along with a better nose, breasts, muscle tone, legs. It's great to care for your body but care for it's own sake, not to have a better body than others. Respect your body as part of you, not as a machine that you must drive and control.

Body obsession makes real interpersonal communication difficult. How can you focus upon others while looking in the mirror? How can you achieve intimacy while dwelling upon how well you're performing? The result is unmet interpersonal needs, loneliness, emptiness, despair. So, in addition to accepting your body, obsessors also need to become more honestly involved with others. What are the people around you thinking? Feeling? Doing? Wanting? You may also have to accept other people's bodies as they are rather than criticizing too much and only noticing bodily flaws.

Finally, you may be compulsive as well as obsessive about your body or sexuality. If so, you may exercise mercilessly, diet religiously, and sexualize everything you do. You feel driven and controlled by your compulsions, but you haven't been able to stop. You may well need to seek help, either from a professional or from a self-help group because you may not be able to solve this serious problem on your own. But you can begin the process by focusing on the concept of moderation in all things. Exercise is fine—in moderation. So are dieting and sexuality. But too much of anything takes away a person's choices and without choices you lose much of your humanity.

Disgust

When shame and disgust are paired people turn away with revulsion from their own bodies and drives. Obviously, then, healing this kind of shame involves turning toward your body instead of away. Like disowners, it's important for those filled with body shame and disgust to renew their interest in their bodies.

But it takes more than mere curiosity to fix this problem. You have to directly challenge the "ugh, yuck" response that always accompanies body and sexual disgust. The way to do so is by rooting out the sources of this negative response. When, exactly, did you begin to hate your own body? What happened to you? Who told you that your body was bad? When did you start turning away from yourself? Perhaps, for instance, your sexual disgust began in childhood for protection, as a way to deflect inappropriate advances. Maybe someone wouldn't want you if you hated your body or despised the sexual parts of yourself. But today that protection may be unnecessary and outdated. Knowing how you developed your shame may help you now let go of this defense.

What if the source of your body or sexual disgust and shame is rigidly religious or moralistic parents? Then you must separate your loyalty to them from their particular beliefs. Yes, they did the best they could. And yes, they tried to save you from evil. They mixed fear, shame, and disgust in with your sexuality because they distrusted their own impulses as well as yours. Sexuality, to them, was an enemy. That's why they tried to protect you from it. But they hurt you badly in the process, destroying your faith in your own body. Now is the time to retire their fears. You can be both good *and* sexual, because sexuality is a healthy part of you.

What if you grew up with people who regularly called you fat, ugly, unattractive, or disgusting? Worse, what if you're still getting called names like that, perhaps by a spouse or partner who puts you down in order to feel superior? These messages must be expelled. What you are is *human*. You, like every human being, need to hear words of appreciation. You have the right to be treated with respect and dignity. You may need to enlist your anger here to help confront these negative messages from the past or present. You may need to address those who shame you directly, letting them know you've had enough: "No, I will *not* accept your criticism and insults any longer! I am human! I am attractive! I am good enough!" Frankly, if significant people in your life cannot accept that confrontation and continue to treat you disrespectfully, it's time seriously to consider changing your circle of friends and family. You need your self-respect more than you need them.

Exercises

1. Every part of your body is essential to you, and each part of your body works hard and consistently to help you keep functioning as well as can be. When you treat all or parts of your body as objects, you aren't supporting them well in return. The best relationships—including the one with yourself—flourish most with appreciation, good listening, thoughtfulness, and caring. Think for a minute what traits you would like the person closest to you to have. Now ask yourself, who are you closer to than your stomach? Have you been appreciating what it does to nourish all of you, including your brain? Do you listen to your stomach with respect, or ignore the signals it sends you about what it needs? Are you thoughtful about what you eat if your stomach is sensitive or do you just cram any old thing down there? Do you care about your stomach? Are you happy to have it, even when it gets in your way, acts up because of what you put in it, or reminds you that you're human? Or perhaps you don't like it because it sticks out, because you have kept it as full as possible so it won't bother you. Often it is your stomach that will remind you that you're only human, that you are not perfect, and that your body needs attention. What your stomach needs is part of what you need. You will know much more about yourself if you appreciate, listen to, and consider how you relate to your stomach.

   The same is true for other parts of your body. In a sense, your body is an interdependent community of parts. It's also a part of who you are spiritually, emotionally, and mentally, as well as being physical. Let one small part go wrong and see the way consequences affect all these parts of your life.

   Name ten things you like / appreciate / are grateful for related to your stomach.

   > To your face
   >
   > To your hips
   >
   > To your toes or feet
   >
   > To your lips
   >
   > To your kidneys
   >
   > To your breasts and genitals

Take one day and focus on each of the above parts of you in order to notice what that part tells you, and what it needs. Then give your body what it needs according to the signals you have noticed. Do notice whether and how shame comes up during this week of exploration. Have you learned to be ashamed of particular parts of your body? Of even needing anything? Of talking about what you need? Of entering or leaving a group to attend a personal need? Share what you discover about yourself with someone you trust, or write in your journal.

2. How do you obsess about body-related issues? What are the things you worry about most related to your body, and if one of those things changed a little for the better, would that be good enough?

   When people are obsessing about what is wrong with their bodies, it's hard for them to pay attention to others. Everything that occurs is seen through the lenses of their obsession. For example, Mary is feeling ashamed about her body and has been obsessing about being "too fat." She belongs to an athletic club, and goes to exercise. Afterward, she decides to relax in the whirlpool. Soon after she enters, the three other women there climb out and leave. Mary feels relieved that she is alone so no one can see her but also upset, because she thinks they probably left because they didn't want to be around a grotesque person like her. The real truth, of course, was that they had been in long enough already, and were just moving on with their lives. But Mary's obsession both hurts her and makes it likely that she'll take other people's normal behaviors too personally. Have you ever been in this position? When?

   Most people get obsessive at times. Next time you catch yourself thinking obsessively about your body or your health, try the following exercise. Give a different fill-in answer to the following question ten times: If I weren't busy obsessing, I would be

   _____.

3. On a scale of 1 to 10, where 1 is "completely true" and 10 is "completely false," how do you rank yourself on the following checklist?

   _____ I am proud of my sexuality.

   _____ I respect myself for how I conduct my sexual life and behavior.

   _____ I am relaxed about my sexual feelings and impulses.

   _____ I am sexually competent without having to be perfect.

_____ Sexual contact for me is about sharing and not about performance.

_____ I feel comfortable talking about my sexuality with my partner or a close friend.

_____ I feel joy and goodness in sexual contact.

_____ I am discreet in my sexual behavior and feelings.

_____ I am honest about sex and don't use it as a weapon or manipulation.

_____ I am in control of my own sexual behavior, and I can say "yes" and "no" without being swept away by my feelings or other people's wishes.

_____ I respect myself enough to insist on safe sex.

From 1 to 120, how positive is your sexual identity on this checklist? What score would you like to have? What is one change you could make to raise your score?

4. What did you learn about sexuality growing up in your family? Were both sexes equally valued? How has this affected you? What did you learn about sex from your father? What did you learn about sex from your mother? Did you learn that sex and anger or aggression are connected? Did you know that your body was going to change before you hit puberty? How has that affected you? Did you feel free to ask questions about sexuality? Were these questions answered respectfully? Were you punished, ridiculed, or shunned because of your sexual development? What have you learned about sexuality from your partners? Did you learn this verbally or nonverbally, directly or indirectly, in positive words or through blame, disgust, or accusation? What would you really like to hear about your sexuality? What would you like to hear now to feel good about your sexual self and identity? Write the answers to these questions in your journal. Then say the answers to the last two questions to yourself often, and give yourself permission to believe them.

5. Circle one in each group. What could you discover about your sexuality if you let go of the old learning and listened to yourself right now?

Is being sexual more like:

· flying

Is being sexual more like:

· bungee jumping

- swimming
- skating

- tree climbing
- belly laughing

Is feeling sexual more like:

- macaroni and cheese
- prize-winning chili
- hot cocoa

Is feeling sexual more like:

- listening to music
- dancing
- watching the sunset

Which is sexier to you:

- shining eyes
- sleepy eyes
- soft eyes

Which is sexier to you:

- physical vitality
- sharp thinking
- passionate emotions

Is being sexual more like:

- upside down toast and jelly
- building a birdhouse
- taking this quiz

Is being sexual more like:

- Robinson Crusoe
- Alice in Wonderland
- The Tar Baby

Did answering these questions feel odd or embarrassing? If so, why would that be? One reason, of course, is that sexuality is a very private and intimate event. Another could be that your shame may prevent you from really noticing and thinking about what sexuality means to you. Or perhaps your shame is just enough connected with sexuality to keep you from having fun being sexual.

6. Homosexuality is often derided because it threatens many people. Yet about one in ten people is homosexual and many additional persons are bisexual. These numbers don't include those people who briefly experimented with homosexuality during their childhood and early-teen years. Furthermore, each of these sexual states of being may be determined genetically, before a child is even born.

Imagine a conversation between two gay men or lesbian women. One is ashamed of their sexuality; the other has a healthy pride. List four things each has to say:

Shamed person   **Proud person**

_____   _____

_____   _____

_____   _____

_____   _____

If you identify yourself as a person with an alternative sexual lifestyle, which way is closest to the way you feel about yourself? Why? If you identify yourself as a person with a traditional sexual lifestyle, which way is the closest to the way you feel about yourself? Why? Which speaker feels right to you? Why?

The Shame/Rage Connection: How Shame Sparks Violence

What Is Rage?

Rage is more than strong anger. It is violent, furious, passionate, wrathful, frenzied, out-of-control anger. Rage is madness. Here are some examples of what rage sounds like:

- "All of a sudden I become irate. I go ballistic if anyone even hints that I've done something wrong. I just can't stand being criticized."

- "Every time I get a new girlfriend the same thing happens. I start getting real pushy. I want more and more of her time and attention. I get jealous. Needy. Sometimes I get so desperate I hurt her. When one girlfriend goes away I begin the same cycle with the next woman."

- "When I get angry I don't fight fair. I hit below the belt. I don't simply want to make my point. No, I want to destroy my opponent. I want to publicly disgrace them."

While rage is usually associated with feeling angry, many writers (for instance: Morrison 1989; Retzinger 1991; Kaufman 1996; Lewis 1992; Potter-Efron 1989) believe that most rage episodes are really a result of a combination of anger and shame. Because of this shame-anger connection, rage differs even from strong anger in several important ways. Above all, rage frequently follows an insult to one's identity, thus producing shame. Rage is more about a threat to the self, while anger is more a response to the frustration of one's goals or actions. Rage also involves intense deeper feelings of powerlessness, more unconscious processes, less awareness of one's real feelings (especially the shame), less clear focus, and more generalized thoughts (Lewis citing Retzinger 1992) like, "They're always putting me down," or "I can't stand being treated like a child, and that's all they do."

Rage is a major factor in extreme violence. To quote Lewis (1992) describing a police officer's distinction between routine and brutal murders: "In the brutal murders, someone in effect is murdered ten times over. Those murders are likely to be murders of rage." Such savage attacks are most often directed against family or others who intentionally or accidentally attack the perpetrator's sense of self. Feeling intolerably weak or bad, perpetrators lash out at those they believe are trying to destroy them. Although certainly every rage attack doesn't lead to murder, it's important to recognize that rage does inevitably include a wish to destroy.

Rage develops through many stages. Sometimes these stages play out in just a few minutes, sometimes over months. Although we'll describe the stages as if someone were fully aware of what is happening to them, in reality, rage mostly develops deep inside people's minds and is only a partly conscious process. Rage is irrational. That's why ragers frequently don't make sense when they finally scream out in indignation about the intolerable insults they can no longer endure. Their partners might say something like this: "Why, honey, I said that months ago and that's not even what I meant. You mean you've been stewing about that all this time? Why didn't you tell me?" But that might not be enough. Ragers demand abject apology, humiliation, total defeat. Convinced they have been desperately wounded, they try to destroy their enemies.

The Stages of Rage

Stage One: The Five A's

The Five A's are attention, approval, acceptance, admiration, and affirmation. These are basic needs so deeply ingrained that life without them becomes virtually meaningless. These gifts from others, in other words, make people feel fully alive and human.

So what do little children do when they don't get those things? The answer, of course, is that they fly into a rage. Previously adorable infants become monsters, screaming their protests into the air. They become inconsolable, too. Even hugs and kisses can't end their tantrums. Only exhaustion stops these raging youngsters. And do you have any doubt that in the midst of these rages if they only could they would destroy everything and kill everyone in sight, even those whose attention, approval, acceptance, admiration, and affirmation they so desperately desire?

All adults need these same Five A's. They're not something you grow out of as you get older. However, most adults have developed a capacity to tolerate their temporary absence, as long as they don't have to go too long without them. Beyond a certain point, though, almost everybody who feels deprived of attention, approval, acceptance, admiration, and affirmation becomes depleted. They feel weak, powerless, devitalized. People become emotionally starved when they don't get enough of these so called "emotional supplies." Emotional hunger is the breeding ground for emotional desperation and that, in turn, sets the stage for rage.

Every person has a unique need for each of the Five A's. Some people need more attention, others more approval, etc. Also, some adults seem far more needy than others. These individuals always seem to be on the brink of emotional starvation. One reason is that they have difficulty accepting people's gifts of attention, approval, acceptance, admiration, and affirmation. That means no matter how well others try to feed them, they stay hungry. They cannot grow emotionally because of this deficit just as a child with intestinal problems cannot grow physically even when continuously fed. Since a lack of the Five A's increases the likelihood of rage, it's obvious that those people who suffer from this kind of emotional hunger are more rage prone than others.

Stage Two: A Disappointing World

There would be no rage if the only purpose of others, their only reason for existence, was to serve and obey. But that's not their purpose, nor yours. None of us are here just to supply another's needs for the Five A's.

The world occasionally disappoints in two main ways (Morrison 1989). First, significant people may be *unresponsive*. In American society, the stereotyped image for unresponsivity is the father absorbed in his newspaper while his children try unsuccessfully to get his attention. But it's not only fathers who may be unresponsive. So might mothers, grandparents, siblings, friends, colleagues, and lovers, tuning out just when you most want them to tune in to your needs. "Pay attention to me!" you want to shout. "No way, I'm busy with other things," they say or imply. The result may be that you feel unwanted, unloved, and unappreciated.

Rejection may be as much of a problem as neglect. The message of rejection is "Go away. There's something wrong with you." Rejection is more active, more immediately shaming than unresponsiveness or disinterest. It often triggers more powerful shame episodes because there can be no doubt about the other's judgment. You know without question when you are rejected that you have been found defective and deficient. But, in the long run, both disinterest and rejection are powerful threats to someone's self-worth.

Stage Three: Prolonged, Unacknowledged Shame

"There must be something wrong with me. I'm not good enough." These thoughts are a natural reaction to times when the world fails to affirm people, especially children. You decide that the problem must not be with the world and blame yourself. "I'm the problem, not my parents." This is internalized shame, the self judging itself unworthy. But internalized shame is a terribly painful feeling so it often gets buried deep in the unconscious. This strategy only creates more trouble, though, because shame that has been hidden away even from the person feeling ashamed cannot be healed. It festers. It lurks. And, as you'll see, it may easily become converted into rage as shamed individuals unconsciously stew over past disappointments.

Prolonged but unacknowledged shame burdens the soul. The more people suffer this particular indignity, the more they sense that something is painfully wrong inside them. But they fail to identify exactly what it is that so bothers them. Their shame remains hidden from their own awareness because it simply hurts too much to feel it.

What thoughts and feelings would normally accompany this shame? Failure. Emptiness. Weakness. Inferiority. Humiliation. Badness. But these reactions also are intolerable. True, they often hover on the edge of awareness, but they are vigorously defended against. "Empty? No way! A failure? Never! Weak? Absolutely not!" Humiliation, in particular, feels so bad that it is frequently suppressed.

Stage Four: Getting Rid of the Shame

What we're describing are people's determined efforts to save their self-esteem. If they felt this prolonged shame it would devastate them. But sometimes just hiding from shame isn't enough. That shame keeps trying to get out, like a determined genie wanting to escape from its bottle. So now these deeply shamed people must find something else to do with it before it destroys them.

The solution is to displace the shame, to project it away from yourself, to transfer it to others. This isn't the same as giving shame back to the original shamers, though, because that is a fully conscious, healthy process. Instead, shamers begin to think they see in others the exact qualities of which they are most secretly ashamed of in themselves. They exaggerate, too. So, if they are ashamed of their laziness, they accuse their loved ones of being the most slothful couch potatoes known to humankind. Their sense of failure becomes a conviction that others are total washouts. Their emptiness turns into accusations that others have lost their souls. Their shame, however it is manifested within them, is cast out and given away.

Stage Five: A Triggering Event

The stage is now almost completely set for rage. Only one element remains: the need for a triggering event. By now almost anything will do because the person's shame still remains a terrible threat. Yes, now it been given away to another. But even so, the shame is there, palpable and shimmering. As long as there is shame anywhere it could eventually get returned to its owner. The only solution is to destroy the shame. And the only way to do that is to annihilate the person now labeled as shameful.

The trigger for this process is any comment or action that might bring shame back to its original owner. Maybe someone makes a sarcastic remark. Perhaps they say something that might be construed as critical (and surely will by these overly shame-prone persons). Or maybe the trigger is created out of thin air. That happens when people imagine they are being belittled when there is no evidence of that at all.

The alleged insult triggers rage. The shame must be eradicated *right now*, before it gains a foothold in the shamed person's consciousness. Shame and anger become magnified, intensified. The insult becomes a humiliation that cannot and will not be tolerated in the rager's mind. Irrational thinking takes place as well: "If I can destroy you forever then I can destroy my shame forever." Notice we're definitely not talking about simply defeating one's shame but *annihilating* it. That can only be done by annihilating one's enemy, either psychologically or physically. Only then can the person's shame be expunged.

Stage Six: Attack

The attack that follows may be verbal, physical, or both. Whatever the means, it will surely be violent—the interpersonal equivalent of a tornado or hurricane. The goal, after all, is to destroy the shame that has been projected onto the other. No wonder, then, that ragers hurl the nastiest insults they can think of. And, when they attack physically, it is often with primitive "biting" violence. These ragers are attempting to eradicate their shame. But no matter how successful their assault, they can never fully succeed because they are attacking the wrong target. Their shame is really inside *them*, no matter how hard they try to convince themselves otherwise. So they attack and attack again. Their rage may turn fatal as they truly destroy their targets, but even that cannot be enough, which is why their anger eventually may be turned into a suicidal rage against themselves.

Stage Seven: Shame/Rage Spirals

Ragers cannot eliminate their shame by raging. But they can and do increase it. Every time they hurt the people they love, their shame increases at some level of consciousness. They feel worse and worse about themselves. But, if they couldn't tolerate the original amount of shame, how could they be expected to tolerate even more? So what can they do? Unfortunately, the answer is more of the same. The greater their shame, the more savagely and frequently they rage. The more they rage and attack the more shame they must endure. This creates a shame/rage spiral into misery. It also ensures continuing conflict with one's family and the world. And, until ragers can break out of this pattern, their chances of making extremely brutal assaults, committing homicide, and attempting suicide will keep increasing.

How to Break the Shame/ Rage Connection

There is a way to break free from this shame/rage linkage. It will take a lot of honesty and a fair amount of sustained effort but, if you identify yourself with this pattern, it could save your life as well as the lives of those you love the most.

Here is the secret to breaking the shame rage connection: You'll need to work *backwards* through the seven stages, beginning with the seventh and ending with the first. Going backwards through the stages is the best way to ensure you won't leave anything out or rush too quickly through it. That way, you can take your time to do it right.

There is one exception to the proceeding backwards pattern. You will need to make an immediate promise not to get violent. So be sure to read through the rest of this chapter before beginning your personal work. By making this commitment you will be able to take the time to understand and change the deeper dynamics that have forged the links between shame and rage.

Catalogue Your Shame/Rage Spirals

The first step calls for careful observation. You'll need to keep a notebook or your journal handy so you can write down the details of how, when, where, how long, and on whom you rage. But notice the absence of the question "why." Don't do "why." It's too early right here to bother with that particular query. You'd probably only come up with blaming statements anyway—it's their fault you rage, not yours. If only they'd do and say what you want then everything would be fine. Asking why, in other words, would only set you up to rage again. But the other questions, the how, when, where, how long, and on whom questions, will supply you with a wealth of vital information.

Start by studying your most recent rage episode. What happened? How did you lose control? What did you say and do? What did you think and feel? You'll need to remember what others said and did as well but don't focus on that. Remember that it wasn't what they said or did that counts so much as how you reacted to them. The shame/rage spiral occurs within you so you'll need mostly to notice your own thoughts and actions.

Then continue backwards in time. Think about past rages. Did they follow almost exactly the same pattern? Were they different? If so, how? Don't ignore the present, though, even while you're studying the past. Notice any shame/rage spirals you fall into now even if they don't result in a full-blown rage.

The goal is for you to become an expert on your personal shame/rage spiral pattern. If you won't be, who will?

Make a Long-term Commitment Not To Rage

Before going any further, we must ask you to make one immediate promise to yourself, *a personal pledge right now to refrain from rage—vicious verbal or physical attack*—while you're learning how to break the shame/rage pattern. The reason we ask you to make this promise is that even beginning to work on your shame and rage can trigger bad feelings inside you. Since you've developed the unconscious habit of attacking when you feel bad, these feelings could be dangerous. More fury is the last thing you need in your life right now, so the only way to stop it is to make an immediate commitment not to rage. Besides, you simply can't keep attacking others and hope to get anywhere with this problem. One reason we say this is that you will need to reclaim your shame to break the shame/rage connection. You can't do that while simultaneously giving it away, which is what happens when you rage at others.

This is a high-stakes promise. After all, every time you rage you put your health and the safety of others on the line. So make every effort to keep this promise. Take a "time-out" if you must by leaving the scene until you feel better. Enlist the help of friends who will help you calm down when you need assistance. You may even have to quit drinking or using drugs if they contribute to the problem. No matter what the provocation, do not give yourself permission to blow. Remember that every rage episode damages yourself and others. The only way to protect everybody's safety is to eliminate these rages.

But don't stop here. Quitting at this point means that you might just be "stuffing" your anger and shame instead of dealing with it. For long-term gain you'll need to continue working backwards through the shame/rage stages.

Learn What Triggers Your Rages

There are two kinds of triggers for shame and rage. The first are the words and deeds of others (as you interpret them). The second are things you say to yourself that make you furious. Certainly the two interact a lot. But let's look at them one at a time right now.

Possibly everybody has a few "Whatever you say don't say that about me" vulnerabilities. "Don't say I'm mean." "Don't say I'm dumb." "Don't say I'm too nice." "Don't say I'm an alcoholic." "Don't say I'm a coward." These are external triggers, the words you dread because they trigger shame. Others might not even know that these words are taboo. They might say them without malice. But whether intentional or not, hearing those phrases makes you fume. "How dare they say that about me? They have no right. Those stupid, idiotic jerks! They ought to be taught a lesson." Boom! One rage episode coming up as you become enraged and try to shame those who have just shamed you. You're not just a little angry, either. If it's a real rage, your goal is to destroy those bastards before they can say another word.

Internal triggers are trickier than external ones. These are the half-conscious phrases you tell yourself that add to your shame. "I'm a fool. I'm not as smart as others in this class. I'll never succeed. I'm fat. I'm ugly. I'm not good enough." These internal insults sometimes develop out of the blue. That's when people start calling themselves names for no particular reason. They may also occur in the face of failure or frustration. That's when you might scold yourself for being incompetent.

Here's how internal and external triggers interact. Frequently, an external trigger jump-starts an internal trigger. Someone else says or implies that you're not very graceful and you think something like this: "They're right. I am so clumsy. I'm probably the clumsiest person alive. Boy, do I feel like a fool." The pattern can also be reversed so that an internal trigger encourages an external one. You might, for instance, believe that you're a phony who doesn't deserve to be a teacher, plumber, parent, etc. That's your secret shame. But, because you think that about yourself, you become excruciatingly sensitive to anything others might say that might validate your fears. So, if a fellow teacher mentions that your class is one day behind theirs in reading, you take that as a sign that your colleague really believes you are a lousy instructor.

Take some time to think carefully about your external and internal triggers. What do others say or do that triggers your shame? What self-shaming thoughts do you have?

Quit Giving Away Your Shame/ Reclaim Your Shame

We've combined stages three and four of the shame/rage process because they represent flip sides of the same coin. On one side, ragers cannot admit they feel shame. On the other, they try to give their shame away to others so as to distance themselves from it as much as possible.

The shame/rage spiral depends upon people playing hot potato with their shame—throwing it to someone else as quickly as they can because it's too hot to hold. But you cannot heal your shame by running away from it. No matter how far you throw it from you it always returns. So it's critical that you quit transferring your shame. It certainly doesn't do them any good to receive it and it definitely keeps you from feeling better about yourself. That means every time you want to shame another person you'll need to stop yourself and ask one essential question: "Right now am I saying something to someone else that I really believe about myself?" Are you calling someone else ugly when it's yourself that feels ugly? Are you claiming another is dumb only because you don't want to think about your latest less-than-brilliant actions?

It's time to reclaim your shame. It's yours, after all, nobody else's, and nothing good can occur until you take back that which rightfully belongs to you. You must acknowledge the unacknowledged, admit the inadmissible, and accept the unacceptable about yourself, not to suffer but to heal. You'll need courage to approach that which has been avoided. Just remember that your shame is not an enemy. It's part of you.

There's one more idea that might help you here. Shame thrives in the psychological darkness of denial but shrinks in the daylight of full consciousness. The more you address your shame the less scary it will be. Besides, that's the only way to break the shame/rage connection. As bad as shame sometimes feels, it won't trigger your rage as long as you stay completely aware of it. That puts you in control of your shame instead of the other way around.

Trace Your Disappointment History

We've noted that there are two kinds of interpersonal disappointments that lead to shame. The first are times when important people are unresponsive to your needs. The second is when they more actively reject you. It's important for you to think seriously about how and when you've been disappointed in these ways both recently and in your past. Be careful, though, to search your history for useful information, not in order to blame others for your pain.

You'll want to look for patterns as well as individual events. It's not only that Dad kept reading his newspaper one night when you wanted to play with him. It's that you were often ignored by your parents and siblings, even when you were sick or needy. These patterns create templates in people's minds such as becoming convinced that you will have to fight for people's attention the rest of your life and that any lack of attention is shameful and therefore completely unacceptable.

Try neither to minimize nor exaggerate while you note your disappointment history. Just focus on gathering information that will help you understand yourself better.

Attend to Your Current Need for the Five A's

Attention. Approval. Acceptance. Admiration. Affirmation. Everyone needs their share of each of these precious gifts. But which do you need the most? Which do you hunger for? Which do you sense you didn't get enough of when you were younger?

Emotional starvation can lead to desperate action. That's why you need to know which of these needs you most hunger for now. It's exactly those needs that precipitate the shame/rage process when unmet. "I need your . . . (attention, approval, etc.). But you're not giving it to me. I feel awful. I feel ashamed. I hate you. I want to destroy you." Perhaps now, knowing what you need from others, you'll be more able to ask for it. Also, when you don't get it, you'll be more able to accept your disappointment without flying into a rage.

It's possible that your basic need for one or more of the Five A's has become shame bound. If so you'll feel shame whenever you feel the need for affirmation, admiration, or the like. But now you can challenge this useless shame. Just remember that it's absolutely normal to want and need all five A's.

The key to preventing another shame/rage episode is to stay aware of your wants and needs. That doesn't mean you'll always get them met immediately, of course. A certain amount of disappointment is inevitable. But knowing your wants leads to asking to get them met and to being able to accept disappointments as they arise without feeling shame or rage.

Watch for Signs of Relapse

Finally we suggest that you watch carefully for any signs that the shame/rage pattern is building up again. Shame is a sneaky emotion. It seldom announces itself over your brain's loudspeaker. It's all too easy to relapse into rage even when you think you're doing well. You might want to keep a list of the signs of building rage in your purse or wallet. You also need to trust others by asking them to inform you if they are noticing any danger signs. And don't "pooh pooh" them if they do share their concerns. You can't afford to ignore any evidence that you're heading back into rage.

The shame/rage connection leads to violence and misery. But it can be broken.

Exercises

1. The shame/rage connection is a tough one to address if you are the angry shamer yourself. Part of the reason is that you have developed that shame/rage connection to defend yourself against feeling worthless, small, weak, inadequate, or defective in some way. What better solution than anger to make you feel self-justified, bigger than life, more than adequate to judge others, and in good shape compared to those you're criticizing for being defective. The biggest problem, of course, is that you are not a courageous fighter, but a cowardly lion acting as if you were not. Unthinking rage is nothing to be respected. At most it generates fear, hate, resentment, revenge, and exactly the kinds of shame in others that hurt you so much.

   The first leg of this triathlon is allowing yourself to stay human-sized instead of using your anger to help you get bigger than life (and as Pat's dad would say, half as natural). Think about it. What if someone said something you could take offense at, and instead of getting ready to blow up, you politely checked out how the person intended what he said. Or checked out whether they were having a tough time, feeling grumpy or anxious. That reverses the process of them just worrying about you, it's true. You might get less attention just then. But you would have allowed yourself to be just a normal, everyday human being; you would have established a sense of equality with the other person; and you would have a lot to respect yourself for. Our hunch is that the attention you would receive over time would actually be warmer, more respectful, and more genuine if you could separate your fears from other people's behavior. Practice checking our what people really mean by what they say, instead of jumping to conclusions, or assuming—which, as one twelve-step group points out, can make an "ass" of "u" and "me."

Use deeper breathing to calm your anxiety while you learn how to trust others a little more by finding out what they mean, as opposed to what you *think* they mean. Breathe a little deeper for the next week and practice checking things out by saying one of the following:

- Excuse me. Could you rephrase that?
- I don't think I quite got your meaning.
- What are you thinking about in terms of that?
- I'm not quite sure what you mean. Tell me again.

2. One way to get rid of excessive shame is to become overly critical of others—to humiliate them before they humiliate you. To find out how much of this you have learned, try to answer these questions as honestly as you can:.

- Do you enjoy being "one up" on others?
- Do you generally feel superior to those around you?
- Do you prefer to control your husband/wife/friends/children?
- Do you tend to pick at others' faults?
- Are you known as hard to please by others?
- Do you feel better about yourself when others fail?
- Do you get disgusted with those around you?
- Do you believe a good offense is the best defense?
- Do you criticize others but resent being criticized?
- When you're mad at somebody, do you see them as all bad?
- Do you feel morally right and justified when you're angry?

Was there anyone in your life who has treated you in these ways? If so, who? If you continue the way you're acting right now, what do you think the epitaph on your tombstone will be? What would you like it to be? Do you realize that shaming rage really harms others? Do you know that it creates physical changes in you that will literally shorten your life? This is the second leg of that triathlon—understanding that you do not have to get mad to have an impact on other people, and that if you learn to listen carefully, usually no one needs to be humiliated at all, because they can speak as equals and understand each other.

3. Here's the third leg of the race that gets you to the final ribbon—a decision to do something besides blow up. Notice what thoughts you have just before you get triggered. Watch for regular thoughts such as: "I don't have to put up with this." "They can't do this to me." "Who do they think they are?" "They don't deserve my being nice to them." or, "How come I don't get any respect around here?" When you identify a pattern of thought that comes right before you fly off the handle, learn to take a time-out right then. For example, when our kids were quite young, Ron found himself getting mad at them pretty often. As he listened to his thoughts, he heard, "I'm really being patient now," just before he blew up. After that, the moment he thought "I'm really being patient now," he got up and took a time-out. Once he'd relaxed a little, he could work things out with them without assuming that they were being intentionally disrespectful.

4. Redefine respect, if that is really what you want. Let respect be that others can trust you enough to tell you the real truth, rather than defining it as being scared enough to be obedient. Act as if the new definition were true, and you as well as others will develop new respect and love for yourself. We know a man who carries a stone in his pocket just to remind him that simple honesty is the best policy because it respects everyone, including himself. Put something in your pocket that reminds you to cherish honesty instead of power.

5. The next few times you get really angry at others for doing something wrong, take some time later to ask yourself what in your own life is the closest you have come to what they did. If that doesn't help you much, ask yourself what they were getting too close to that you didn't want pointed out. If you keep a record of these things, perhaps in your journal, you will discover that often you are "projecting," or thinking that someone else may be doing

or saying something you would be thinking in the same situation, even if you didn't say it. The truth is, you can't read anyone's mind but your own—and to read your own you have to look closely at yourself.

Some people put it this way: Every time you point your finger at someone else, the rest of your fingers are pointing back right at you. Let yourself notice that.

Couples and Families: Shaming and Blaming vs. Mutual Respect

Mutual Disrespect

It's an all too typical meal at the Emersons' dinner table.

> "I won't eat this slop."
> "You're a pig."
> "Yeah, well, you're anorexic."

Insults get passed around the Emerson table faster than bread-sticks. Everybody takes turns, too. Maybe Mom starts by belittling Dad, then one of the kids shames another, then Dad starts attacking, and finally the family finishes their meal with cold food and a cold silence. Each person scores "victories" along the way by saying things that make another feel really bad. Reducing Mom to tears scores big points. So does driving Dad into a rage, getting Joey to stutter, Marti to throw up, or Terrence to march away from the table without eating. Shame and blame is the name of this game. Unfortunately, it produces no real winners. Rather, just about everyone who lives in families like the Emersons' suffers from lowered self-esteem, feelings of incompetence, distrust of others, enduring resentments, and a tendency to disrespect exactly those people they most love.

Mutual disrespect is the hallmark of shame-based couples and families. Mutual disrespect is a set of negative choices people make:

- to criticize rather than praise;

- to interrupt instead of listening;

- to ignore when someone needs attention;

- to nitpick and fault find rather than look for the good;

- to not allow difference rather than appreciate each person's uniqueness;

- to point out family members' faults in public when a private conversation would be far less humiliating;

- to keep making shaming comments that tell family members that they are no good, not good enough, unlovable, incompetent, worthless, and bad.

Please notice our emphasis upon the two words "mutual" and "choices." "Mutual" is important because we're talking here about couples and families in which just about everyone participates in shaming and blaming each other.

True, there are couples and families with only one shamer, usually a bully who uses shaming and blaming to gain power and control over others. We call this situation a "one-way" shaming relationship. This kind of behavior works because shaming makes people feel small and weak. There are two basic ways to challenge this pattern. Either those who are being shamed must confront the shamer and insist upon respectful treatment or they may have to just get away. If you think you're in a one-way, disrespectful relationship, either as shamer or shame receiver, this chapter will help you better understand what's happening. But the main focus of this material is on how couples and families develop mutual disrespect so that at least two persons engage in shaming and blaming behaviors. We call these "two-way" shaming relationships, because between these two persons the arrows of shame and blame point in both directions.

Two-way shaming relationships are mutually antagonistic. Sadly, they bring out the worst in people. This is pretty easy to understand, though. People at perpetual war don't tend to fight fair, not when the goal is to defend your honor while attacking the other person's dignity and pride. Keep doing this for a while and people turn ugly. They forget how to praise and appreciate each other. Nor do they dare accept anything nice others in these families may say. Those apparently sweet words (such as "You look pretty tonight . . .") might just be a setup for an insult (". . . for once. Why don't you take better care of yourself?"). You don't have to get suckered this way very often before you shutter the windows of your heart instead of opening the door when you hear the beginning of this kind of false praise.

"Choice" is another critical word. We emphasize it because we strongly believe that disrespectful relationships can be changed into mutually respectful ones. The secret in making this change is substituting positive interactions for negative ones. But we don't mean being nice for a few days or a couple of weeks. These choices must be long-term. They have to last at least a few months before people really believe them. Mutual respect does eventually grow into mutual trust. It just takes time, patience, and consistency.

Disrespectful families differ in how they shame each other. Some families are chaotic and unpredictable. One person might turn against another at any time. One minute Jay's picking on Ned, the next Ned's mimicking Mom, then Dad joins in the action by telling them all they're an embarrassment to his family name. The only certainty in families like this is that at any moment someone will be attacking someone else.

Other families make relatively permanent alliances. The males against the females; the parents against the kids; Mom and Willard against Dad and Marianne. People in each alliance are honor bound to leap to the defense of their allies and to attack the other side. The result is a series of quickly escalating fights as these family warriors get launched into battle. It may have begun because one person tries to protect their ally from another. But after a while, everyone is involved much of the time.

Some families practice scapegoating. A scapegoat is a single individual who gets targeted for most or all of the shaming. The real animal scapegoats in Jewish tradition were literally cast into the desert bearing the sins of the people. Human scapegoats may suffer virtually the same fate by being thrown out of their families. But often they are kept around because they are so useful. The family scapegoat becomes the family's shame carrier. That way the rest of the family can feel pure and good about themselves. They feel no shame because they've given it all to the scapegoat. Chances are, if that scapegoat is banished or leaves on their own, another family member will take over the role. That's all the more reason to keep the current scapegoat around. This sounds very cynical. But we are not saying that people do this consciously. If you are the "black sheep," of your family, you probably feel that you can't do anything right—so why try? But neither you nor the rest of your family understand that in some ways this is a "family job" that has been assigned to you, either temporarily or permanently. Families with scapegoats are usually not conscious of how this has happened and think the scapegoat has done all of it himself. That, of course, is the problem. When people stop looking at themselves it becomes much easier to hurt others without knowing they are doing it.

Disrespectful Couples

Why would two perfectly sane people spend tons of time and energy courting each other and say they're in love only to then continually shame and blame their partners? Why do they turn their lovers into enemies? Why do they sabotage their natural desire for sexual and emotional intimacy by saying and doing things that only drive their mates away? Why do they turn love into hate? Why can't they stop this craziness before they lose their companions forever?

Here are three common answers to the questions above. None of the explanations make much sense, though, because disrespecting the people you love is an exercise in absurdity. Still, it's important to try to understand the inner dynamics of this self-sabotaging behavior.

First, the couple may be stuck fighting over power and control. Their communications then become an endless series of arguments. Who controls the checkbook and budget? Who decides where to go on vacation? Whose family will they live near? Basically, who is in charge of this relationship? Couples stuck fighting over power view their partners as opponents. Shaming and blaming then become powerful weapons they can use to weaken the other person. Why negotiate with an equal when you can dictate your terms to an inferior?

Second, one or both partners may fear real intimacy. Emotional vulnerability is too scary. They literally fear losing their identities if they get too close. They must think of ways to back their partners away so that they aren't swallowed up. What better way to accomplish this than by shaming and blaming your partner? If you hurt them often enough they will eventually retreat. Keep attacking them and finally they won't even try to get close anymore. Instead, they too will probably get into shaming and blaming, joining you in mutually disrespectful communication.

Third, shaming the other person may be an attempt to hide from and give away your own shame. "I'm not stupid, you are." "I'm not lustful, you are." "I'm not lazy, you are." This defense against shame is called projection. It is used unconsciously when it would hurt too much to feel your own shame. Who better to give your shame away to than your partner? After all, your mate is always around. By making your partner into a walking garbage dump, you can discard your shame immediately whenever it threatens.

Whatever the initial causes, disrespect only breeds more disrespect over time. Couples develop the habit of shaming and blaming each other. Love, admiration, affection, joy, trust, and especially respect are gradually driven out of the relationship. The result is that mutually disrespectful couples live mutually unhappy lives.

From Disrespect to Respect

Shaming couples and families can change. To do so you'll need to do two apparently simple things: stop the bad stuff (the shaming and blaming) and start some good stuff (praise and taking responsibility for your own actions). But what looks easy sometimes is not. It may take a lot of patience and effort over a long time before you and your partner or you and your family regularly treat each other with mutual respect. The trick here is to have faith. Don't get discouraged by an occasional slipup either by you or others. Above all, keep a steady hand on the wheel as you steer your ship toward the goal of shared dignity. Also, remember to maintain your commitment not to shame others no matter what they say and do. Your refusal to join will almost certainly make the game of shaming and blaming a lot less enjoyable for others to play. Maybe then they, too, will choose to put that particular game aside.

We've divided the rest of this chapter into two major sections. First, we want to discuss the topic of respectful parenting. That's because we firmly believe mutually respectful families only happen when parents demonstrate how to treat each other and their children with honor and dignity. Yes, children do need to respect their elders. But how can they do that until they've been shown what respect really is? They need their parents to model the what, how, when, and where of respectful behaviors. The more often children see this kind of positive modeling, the better they will get at being respectful themselves.

The second section will be just for couples. What can each member of a partnership do to make their relationship more respectful and less shaming?

Respectful Parenting

Respectful parenting involves much more than merely not shaming your children. It is a set of positive behaviors that tell youngsters they are good, good enough, lovable, that they belong in the family, and that it's wonderful that they exist. Respectful parenting cannot guarantee that children will grow into self-respecting adults or that they will enjoy trouble-free lives. Too many other factors complicate their lives to ensure that future. However, parents who practice respectful parenting will know they have helped create an atmosphere in which their children have the best opportunity to learn that they are valued members of the human community.

We believe that most parents can learn to treat their children with respect, even if they haven't done so before. Perhaps, as you've been reading this chapter, you've become aware of ways in which you shame or fail to respect your children. This realization may make you feel terrible, but it won't do your kids much good for you to feel tremendously guilty about your behavior. What will help a lot, though, is for you to make a commitment to quit shaming them and to begin treating them with honor and dignity.

One caution: No parent is perfect. Intentionally or not, everyone shames their children from time to time. Remember the words from the *Big Book* of Alcoholics Anonymous: "We claim spiritual progress, not spiritual perfection" (Alcoholics Anonymous 1976: 60). Perhaps you could let yourself seek parenting progress instead of perfection. The goal is to learn how to substitute respectful parenting practices for shame-generating ones whenever you can.

It's also important to recognize that healthy children can and will feel shame occasionally. That shame, if it's moderate in intensity and doesn't last too long, may guide them toward greater self-respect and appreciation of others. It will help them gain awareness of their personal boundaries and of the limits of the human condition. Healthy shame allows the development of privacy and intimacy as well. The job of a parent here is to recognize when their children feel ashamed and to offer acceptance and interest during those moments. Parents may not be able to take away all their children's shame but they can demonstrate that they will never abandon them. In that way parents can help their children learn that shame is survivable.

Here are some of the most important ways you can practice respectful parenting.

Replace Deficiency Messages with Respectful Messages

The main deficiency messages parents give their children are that the kids are not good, not good enough, unlovable, that they don't belong in the family, and that they shouldn't exist. These messages promote shame since they are being given by the most important figures in a child's life.

Children need to hear that they are good. We're not referring to approval of their behavior, such as getting high grades, doing good work, or having nice manners. We mean that they need to know their parents appreciate their inner goodness—that the simple fact that they're alive is a great gift to the family. Children who receive this message come to believe their lives have purpose and meaning. They feel wanted for who they are as well as for what they do.

Many positive messages are nonverbal. Parents convey a sense of inner goodness to their children through their smiles, touch, sounds, and looks. So, it's important to attend not just to what you say but to how you say things. Remember that a nasty look nullifies the sweetest words just as a sneer in your voice negates a compliment.

Children also need to be told they are good enough. This means giving praise for their accomplishments instead of criticizing their shortcomings. For example, children who receive a B grade on a test do not merit a long lecture on their lack of ambition. Such lectures only convince children they will never succeed. Rather, their parents could offer praise for their achievement and positive encouragement to do their best on the next test. Since most children have a built-in desire to become competent (see our book entitled *Being, Belonging, Doing*), it is both unnecessary and destructive to focus upon their deficiencies. That kind of treatment is only likely to reduce their drive toward competence and replace it with doubt about their abilities.

Children need to feel that they are deeply loved. Remember that the fear of abandonment lies at the center of the shame experience. Only certainty about being loved can ease this life-threatening terror. Furthermore, your love must be consistent. Parents who seem to love their children one day but not the next contribute to their children's anxiety and uncertainty. On the other hand, parents who remind their children every day, verbally and nonverbally, that they are loved help them believe both that they are loved and that they are lovable. People who go into the world with that conviction are far more confident than those convinced they aren't worth loving.

Children must sense that they have a safe place in their families. They need to feel that they belong. It's critical that no child be ignored or scapegoated because of their personalities or characteristics. Parents need to allow for individual uniqueness by encouraging each of their children to develop their own interests.

Finally, children must hear that they have a right to exist. More than that, they need to feel celebrated and welcomed into the world. They need to learn from their parents that they are no mistake and that their lives have value and meaning. Perhaps this is the greatest gift a parent can give their children—the gift of enthusiastic reception into this world.

Be Understanding

Take the time to try to understand what your children are thinking and saying. Be curious about who they are and who they are becoming. Allow them to be themselves and take pride in their developing independence. Remember that children are not born simply to be like their parents. Your respecting their individual differences will help them feel valued as unique human beings.

Praise Instead of Criticize

Don't be miserly with your praise. Be sure to tell your children what they do that pleases you and also to praise the things they do that helps them feel proud and competent. For example, the parent who gets interested in their child's comic book collection certainly encourages that child to read more than the parent who belittles comic books because they aren't "real" books.

Some parents use shame to try to control their children. True, "shame on you" may work to keep kids in line. But too much shame does tremendous damage to children's sense of self. Praise does no damage to children, and it works at least as well as shame to get children to do or not do things. That's another reason we stress giving children praise instead of shame.

Be Patient

Children need time to grow. They need your permission to make mistakes along the way so they know they don't have to be perfect. For instance, four-year-olds learning to tie their shoes often take forever to get dressed. Then they walk even more slowly than usual since they must stop to retie their shoes about every ten steps. Sometimes parents simply can't take the time, of course. When they can, though, they demonstrate that they respect their children enough to allow them the time they need.

Be Honest

Shame and secrecy are great companions. Nonshaming parents respect their children's privacy. They also keep some things to themselves in the name of their own right to privacy. However, they make a policy of letting their children know about major events affecting any members of the family. It's important, though, to remember that the definition of "major event" varies with age. Great-grandma's death might be much less distressful to a three-year-old than the death of the family's pet hamster.

Be honest with your children and with people who are around you when your children are there. If that crimps your talking style, so be it. Children need the regular example of being honest to understand that a big part of respect is telling the truth. We think it is more respectful for a child to disagree with what we ask of them so that we can talk it over, than for that child to agree and just obey, or even to disobey convinced we are wrong about what we've asked of them. "Do as I say, not as I do," is the epitome of disrespect. "Do as you see me do," enables a child to respect himself, to respect the parent model he is following, and to learn courtesy and honesty in human relationships. "Do as you see me do," is a better way to teach respect than "Do as I tell you because I told you to." However, it's a real challenge for parents, because to follow that road means you have to be all that you can be. It's work, but don't you want to teach your kids to do that, too?

Reassure Your Children That You'll Return

Small children often dread the small abandonments that occur when their parents go away even for a few hours. This fear is genetic and not the fault of the parents. Nor can parents just refuse ever to leave their children—to do so only increases their children's dependency upon them. What parents can do is to patiently reassure their children that they are loved and that they aren't being abandoned. At least a few minutes to celebrate reunions should also be scheduled in whenever possible. Parents who take time to reassure and reunite help their children feel loved both in the presence and absence of those they love.

Treat Children with Dignity

Few parents would enjoy being patted on the head or told that their thoughts were cute or silly. One cartoon we saw has two children being patted on the head and saying to each other that it'll be hard to get any real attention until they hit five feet tall, at least. Respectful parents pay serious attention to their children's ideas and concerns. They neither ignore them nor treat them condescendingly. These parents also keep in mind that children's pride is easily damaged by belittling remarks. Children who are treated with dignity and respect are more likely to grow up both to treat others respectfully and to believe they are worth being treated well by others.

Parents Also Deserve Respect

Respectful families expect every family member to honor the others. Parents lead the way by modeling this behavior. Unfortunately, children don't always graciously follow along. They can be quite rude to their parents. They may swear, disobey, and ignore their elders. Children are not automatically nonshaming.

How should parents respond to these tests? First, it's important to do just that: respond rather than react. Parents who simply react to their children's disrespectful actions will probably counterattack with their own shaming words and deeds. That simply won't help. The goal is to stop excessive shaming, not to reinforce it by demonstrating that kind of behavior.

Smaller children are the easiest to steer toward respect. Parents need to tell them regularly that they can ask for what they want without screaming or name calling. Children don't need long lectures or physical punishment (both of which increase shame) but they may need time-outs or other short disciplines if they don't comply. Most children learn quickly to be respectful, however. That's because they usually feel a whole lot better in a respectful family than a shaming one. Children may need to learn why they are being disrespectful. We have a grandson who is four who was talking back to his dad about eating his dinner. He was being very disrespectful. When he was asked why he was talking to his daddy that way, he said, "Because he tells me things I don't want to hear." He understood very well that he was defending himself. He knew he wasn't being "nice" or respectful. The next step is for him to understand that he doesn't have to be mean because he's hearing something he doesn't like. He has to learn that he can talk about it and decide what to do about it with his dad, and he hasn't mastered all that yet. He's still four, and there's a lot he doesn't know about himself and the world yet. He's lucky that he has a dad who will help him learn with patience. It's important to remember that small children do not have the understanding and abilities that adults have, and that often they are doing the best they can. What may look like intentionally bad behavior may just be the best they can figure out so far.

Adolescents and young-adult children are a greater challenge, especially if they've been previously raised in disrespectful environments. Many teenagers go through periods where they view their parents with barely disguised or undisguised contempt. This represents, partly, a stage in life during which children reject parental and societal values so they can find out what they believe in. Most of these children eventually return to their parents' values. But even if they don't, it's important not to take their actions too personally. They are seeking the meaning of their lives more than they are trying to shame or humiliate their parents.

Nevertheless, children and adolescents should not be allowed to criticize and condemn their parents forever. No parent should have to tolerate verbal or physical abuse from their children. The best response, if there are two parents involved, is a united front in which the youth is informed clearly that shaming words and actions will not be tolerated any longer. Single parents don't have this opportunity for united action. On the other hand, they have less immediate concern that another parent will sabotage their efforts. In either case the message parents must deliver is that they'll be happy to listen and negotiate with their children as long as they state their concerns in a respectful manner. A parent can also ask for respect by being thoughtful before they make decisions, and then sticking to the decisions they have made. If you're going to change your mind, do it right away, not after you child has been badgering you and calling you names. To change your mind because a child is behaving disrespectfully reinforces them to continue to behave that way.

Try not to react to children's shaming maneuvers with shaming actions of your own. The best way to help your children learn to be respectful is to consistently treat them with dignity. It's better to take a position like, "There are certain decisions I must make for this family, and this is one of those decisions," than to fight back by belittling or shaming them. Often, they are caught between belonging in their family and belonging with their peer group, and shaming them will only make the situation worse for both of you.

Respectful Partnership

Many relationships are shame based. That means the partners in the relationship spend far too much time shaming and blaming and far too little praising and accepting each other. We've already described the results of this pattern: Both partners usually feel bad about themselves, their partners, and the entire relationship.

The goal is to become a respect-based partnership. This can only happen by minimizing shaming attacks and maximizing positive interactions. It may be difficult to keep this goal in mind at all times, especially when you're angry with or feel hurt by your partner. But the payoff is tremendous. It simply feels wonderful to be in a mutually respectful relationship.

We've compiled an intentionally brief number of the most important ways that partners can respect each other. However, each relationship is unique. Each couple who reads the following sections may need to add a couple of specific items that would really help to make their relationship feel respectful.

Stop the Shaming

Make a commitment to quit shaming your partner regardless of their behavior toward you. This really comes first. What we mean is that respectful partnership begins with you and only you. Perhaps your partner will also quit shaming and attacking, maybe not. But in either case you can start modeling responsible and respectful behavior. It's important *not* to bargain about this: "I'll quit shaming you if you quit shaming me." The usual result of that bargain is each partner scrutinizing the other's words and actions for any sign of disrespect. Rather, keep your mind on your own words and actions. After all, they're the only ones you can really control.

Act with Respect

Don't look for things to criticize, ignore your partner, make sarcastic remarks, call each other names, threaten to hurt, or actually attack your partner. These are some of the most shaming and disrespectful things people do to each other. Every act of disparagement like these damages your relationship. They destroy trust and build resentments. They also make people feel ashamed and angry, a sure formula for the creation of rage.

Express Appreciation

Do look for things to appreciate in each other and regularly give praise. First you have to notice the goodness in the other. Then you have to let them know that you've noticed. Combine those two, and you help your partner feel significant, competent, loved, and respected. And, as a bonus, the better they feel about themselves and the relationship, the more likely they are to be nice to you.

Remember These Important Facts

- My partner has the right to express their ideas and feelings. That doesn't make them dumb or bad even if they happen to disagree with me.

- My partner has the right to their own likes and dislikes, interests, and hobbies. People in respectful partnerships accept each other's differences.

- My partner wasn't placed on this planet only to meet my needs. He or she has their own wants and needs that I must respect.

- My partner has the right to make mistakes. Screwing up doesn't make them horrible, it just means they're human.

- My partner has the right to be listened to and taken seriously. Ignoring them, laughing them off, or dismissing their legitimate concerns is disrespectful.

- My partner needs to feel worthwhile as much as I do. The goal is to find ways we can both feel good about ourselves rather than fight it out to see who can feel better than the other.

- Above all, my partner has the right to be treated with respect. I can choose consistently to honor that right.

Exercises

1. Stopping a habit of criticism is very difficult. It seems almost second nature to watch what the other person is doing wrong when you have been working from disrespect for quite a while. In order to stop the bad stuff, you must make a decision to stop and find a way to do it. Here is something that will work if you really want it to.

   There's an old rule for feedback that says: If you're going to make a criticism, you must find three positive things first. We have used this at times in our family, as well as in other settings. What this rule means is that in order to earn the right to say one negative thing to your partner, you must find three positive things in what they are doing and tell them about those first. At first, this may be very hard to do. But because it's a task that requires concentration in the beginning, it will help take your attention away from uncomfortable feelings for a bit. If you can't find three real things to praise in your partner, then you may not make your criticism, either. That's the rule.

   When you first try it, you may hate it. It may feel very artificial, as most new behaviors do. But as you do it over time, whether or not your partner does it, you'll notice that it gets easier—and that your attitude toward your partner may begin to change because you've started actively looking for good things about them. Chances are that your partner's attitude toward you will change too. After all, you are now appreciating them more often than you're criticizing.

   The biggest problem in shaming, blaming, and disrespectful marriages is that neither partner believes the other is on their side. In a respectful marriage, both partners know this almost all the time. It doesn't hurt so much to take a criticism from someone you know has your best interests at heart; taking it from someone who seems to be against you, almost an enemy, is much harder. But no one who praises you three times for each one time they criticize is an enemy. Stopping the bad stuff means deciding not to criticize if you're not able to be on the other person's side, as well.

2. In this chapter we have pointed out many problems. However, starting the good stuff is easier if you have some "do's" instead of just "don'ts." All behavior that is stopped has to be replaced with

new behavior—or it just pops up again. Here are some do's for talking to your partner. Try these rules on your own with every family member. If you are patient instead of inconsistent, over time you will see a change in the behavior of every other person.

- **Do** make eye contact without staring.
- **Do** listen instead of interrupting.
- **Do** sit, lean back, lower your voice a little.
- **Do** check out what others are thinking instead of assuming you can read their minds.
- **Do** be respectful instead of rolling your eyes or making faces.
- **Do** take time-outs when you need them, and relax during those time-outs rather than preparing what you want to say back.
- **Do** stay out of others' family relationships with each other. They will figure out how to handle them, if you stay out of the middle.
- **Do** notice the talents and skills of those in your family.
- **Do** breathe deeply instead of holding your breath. Holding your breath increases anxiety and can trigger more shame/rage.

3. When the going gets tough, the tough choose wisdom. Put ten helpful sayings in a box in your sock drawer. Go choose one without looking, read it, and accept it as a message for the day when things get tough. Your sayings could include some of these.

- You are able to learn from everything you do.
- It is the little tyrants in our life who teach us our own character.
- Gratitude expands a person.
- Better never than nasty.
- Even a rotten apple has seeds that grow.
- Why be surprised that no one understands you, when you do not understand yourself yet?
- Laughter heals the soul.

Shame: The Fuel
of Addictions

Shame and Addiction:
Natural Partners

Shame and addiction are natural partners. That's because it's very
hard for shame-based people to soothe or comfort themselves in
times of stress. One client put it this way: "I'm ashamed of myself. I
just go from one addiction to another. First it was booze, then drugs.
Then I quit those things but started eating everything in sight. Now
I'm in trouble with gambling. Every time I lose control I feel like an
idiot. But the worse I feel about myself the more I lose control. I'm
trapped in a nightmare that never ends."

While less shamed persons can remind themselves that they are
basically good, worthwhile, and loved, more chronically shamed people are pummeled by thoughts that they are bad, worthless, and
unlovable. Failing to find any way to soothe themselves and not
believing that anybody else really cares for them, deeply shamed
people look outside of themselves for relief. They seek nothing less

than magic. There must be something out there that will help them feel whole. If not that, at least maybe they can find something that will take away their shame for a little while. And that's exactly where alcohol, drugs, mystical religious movements, food, sex, spending, gambling, work, the latest therapy fad, and so on enter the picture. In their desperation, many deeply shamed persons try out one or more of these potentially addictive or compulsive activities. Will they take away the pain? Will they fill the void that has been created at least partially through shame?

The problem is that the magic works—for a while. Drinkers are warmed by their drinks. Eaters are comforted by their bags of Oreos. Gamblers are so excited by the action that they become distracted from their internal sense of emptiness. Temporarily, all too temporarily, they feel better. They can almost convince themselves that they are human. True, the internal emptiness has only been covered over, not dealt with in a meaningful manner. But perhaps, if that magic lasts, just maybe those horrible feelings will stay away forever. Perhaps this time they have found a way to medicate some of that shame away.

We do want to offer one caution before continuing this discussion. We are not saying here that *all* addictions are caused by shame. Addiction is actually a very complicated process that includes physical craving, genetic predisposition, social expectations, and individual personality characteristics. While we can only concentrate upon the shame/addiction link in this book, we don't want to oversimplify the matter. Shame alone does not inevitably cause addiction any more than addiction inevitably causes shame. However, each typically contributes to the other. Deeply shamed people are high-risk candidates to become addicted, while addicted persons frequently become more and more ashamed of themselves over time. That's why we say that shame and addiction are natural partners.

The Shame/Addiction Spiral

Magic seldom lasts a lifetime. Negative consequences start to build up as people become more and more dependent upon their external source of psychological nourishment. Gradually a negative spiral develops that consists of four main elements: feelings of defectiveness (shame); the use of alcohol, drugs, etc. to escape that feeling; negative consequences; and loss of control. Please look at the illustration called the Shame/Addiction Spiral to see how this process works.

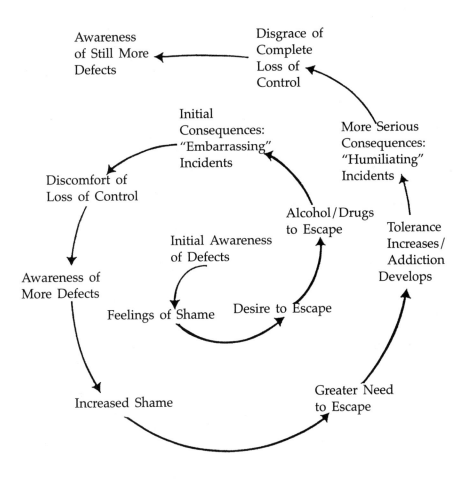

SHAME/ADDICTION SPIRAL

Mary Howell is our name for a woman who has gone through this spiral. Here's her story. Several years ago Mary was nearing the end of a difficult and disappointing marriage. Nobody in Mary's family had ever been divorced. Mary felt like a failure. There must be something about her that was defective. The closer she got to that divorce the worse she felt. Finally, on the very night she signed the final papers terminating the marriage, she found her magic: "I opened a bottle of wine. I drank a couple glasses. And you know what? The pain went away. I felt great. I didn't even think about my failure as a wife or mother." But by the next day the pain was back so Mary drank again. And again. Each time the magic worked for a few hours. But the pain never completely vanished. It was always there, waiting in the background. So Mary kept drinking, gradually developing enough tolerance that she had to drink three glasses instead of two, and then four instead of three.

At first the consequences of her drinking were few. Besides, folks seemed to find it funny when she couldn't find her keys to her car. But that changed over time. Nobody laughed the day Mary got picked up on a drunk driving charge. And Mary certainly didn't find anything humorous about the morning she woke up in a double bed beside some man she didn't even recognize.

Mary's life became a series of disasters. The consequences got worse and worse. They moved from embarrassments to humiliations. Each incident only made Mary feel worse about herself. But by then she only knew one way to feel better and that was to drink even more. It was as if Mary's drinking and her shame were in a race. Mary could stay one step ahead of her shame when she drank enough. But eventually her shame would catch up and she'd have to drink more.

Then there was the shame over losing control. Western society values the idea of always staying in control of our bodies, minds, and emotions. The strong implication is that there must be something wrong with people who can't stay in control. Although Mary resisted admitting she was out of control by denying and minimizing her drinking, still she felt even more like a failure because she simply couldn't quit drinking. She condemned herself all the more because now she felt both weak and bad.

Mary Howell has gotten caught in the shame/addiction spiral. To escape it she will have to do two things. First, Mary needs to quit drinking. But she'll also have to deal with her shame or she'll probably return to drinking or another addiction.

Addiction As a Substitute for Human Relationships

Many addicts seem to live their lives following two simple ideas:

- People are unpredictable. You can't count on them.

- Alcohol, food, drugs, etc., are predictable. They will always be there for you when you need them.

Fear of abandonment lies at the heart of the shame experience: "I never feel safe around people. I always think they'll reject me if I don't say the right words or do the right things. They won't love me. They won't want anything to do with me. Besides, they might abandon me for no reason at all. I don't have any control."

Most people manage their fear of abandonment by believing they are worth loving. They think of themselves as "keepers." They truly think that the important people in their lives appreciate and respect them. Besides, they value consistency. If their partner has stuck with them for months or years they feel confident that their love is secure. However, shame eats away at one's sense of security. The greater your shame the more likely you are to expect to be rejected no matter how unrealistic that fear may be. For example, one deeply shamed woman named Beth once told us, "I still have my mental bags packed" in her marriage, despite being married for over twenty years. She simply could not feel safe. Her self-esteem was so low that she figured any reasonable person would not want to have anything to do with her. Sooner or later she believed her husband George would come to his senses and divorce her.

Beth was a recovering alcoholic. What she liked most about drinking, she said, was that she could rely on her old friend, "Al." Al was always there for her, right there in the refrigerator. Furthermore, Al didn't ask much of her at first, just a few cents a drink and a little of her time. Later, Al turned into an exceedingly jealous lover and demanded she spend almost all her time with him. But even that was all right. By then Beth was drinking alone late at night and sleeping most of the day. She avoided her husband, of course, and complained to Al about how George was unreasonable and demanding. Beth never realized when she was drinking that she basically had abandoned George before he could reject her. Beth's addiction led her to isolation from people. That was the only way she could feel less scared of their rejection.

More Shame/Addiction Connections

Pride and Companionship

"I can drink anyone under the table." That boast by twenty-one-year-old Timothy Edwards might eventually kill him. But not now. Today he feels pride about his awesome ability to consume liquor. A six-pack? Twelve beers? A case? Two cases? Go ahead, name the amount. Tim will show you he can drink beer longer and faster than anyone else.

There are many Tims around proving their consumptive prowess to the world. This process is truly a source of pride to them. For others it's the companionship that counts most. They feel like they really belong after they've had a few drinks, lines, or hits. These people are often a little shy when sober. Their self-esteem isn't too hot either, so they think people won't want to spend time with them. They may not be totally ashamed of themselves, but they always look for something that will help them be a little more outgoing and confident or a little less anxious. Since alcohol or drugs helps give them that lift, they gradually depend on some mood-altering substance to get them over their shyness. Of course, the more they use alcohol and drugs for that purpose the more they learn to depend upon them. They also may convince themselves that they simply can't keep friends, have fun, make love, or relax around people without their substance.

Hiding Shame

"My boyfriend, Harry, feels terrible about his gambling. I'm sure if he could quit he'd feel fine about himself." Maybe. Maybe not. Sometimes the shame about having an addiction or compulsion hides a deeper layer of shame. But the addict, their family, and even their counselors often forget that stopping an addiction is just the beginning of a healing process. True, the addiction itself is the source of much shame and guilt. But there may be much, much more shame in the background. This is the shame many addicted people feel when they believe that they're really useless and worthless. People who quit their addictive behaviors will probably feel good about themselves for that courageous decision. And quitting drinking, using, and other addictions will finally allow addicts to take an honest look at their core shame. But abstinence alone won't cure their core shame.

Distraction from Shame

Preoccupation is one measure of addiction. "When can I drink? Where? With whom? How can I make sure there will be booze at the party? Should I sneak some in the car? How can I keep others from noticing? What will I do if I can't drink?" All these questions occupy the addict's mind. The addiction becomes an obsession. But that's good, because it keeps the shamed person from thinking about some other, much more painful questions: "What's wrong with me?" "Why am I a failure?" "Why don't people like me?" "Why don't I like myself?" The preoccupation with addiction saves addicts from encountering their shame. Unfortunately, the longer they hide from their shame the more scared they get of it. Instead of shame being an uncomfortable emotion it becomes a monster, something that they fear will destroy them if ever faced directly. All of which means that the fear of shame can drive some people to drink as much as the shame itself can.

Achieving Shamelessness

Feelings of shame and guilt are inhibiting. They stop people from saying and doing a lot of things such as shouting at the top of one's lungs, punching holes in the walls, or making inappropriate sexual propositions. But for some people there is a way to take a time-out from shame and guilt. Get drunk. Get stoned. Get high. Now you have a great excuse. "It wasn't me, it was the . . ." We're not saying that disinhibition is always bad, of course. But it should never be used as an excuse for immoral or inappropriate behavior. Besides, sidestepping from shame into shamelessness usually doesn't work for long. Eventually, the sober you will have to face your intoxicated, shameless behavior compounded with all the new shame generated during periods of supposed loss of control.

Proving Shamelessness

Finally, we want to note that some people who feel awful about themselves have a need to demonstrate and prove their shamefulness to others. What better way to do so than getting "s*** faced" drunk, engaging in humiliating sex acts, or getting thrown into jail for prostitution while seeking money for heroin? "See," these people say to all those who might try to care about them, "I'm not worth loving. I'm a total reject. Just leave me alone." Somehow these people flaunt their sense of degradation. They announce to the world that they are shameful beyond repair. They seem only to want to be left alone in their misery.

Shame and Relapse

Why do people so often quit drinking and drugging only to return to these activities despite the clear and obvious suffering their addictions bring to themselves and others? Again, we don't want to oversimplify and say that the reason is always shame. But we do want to suggest strongly that unresolved shame is a major contributor to many people's relapse.

Life is supposed to get better when you break an addiction. People are expected to feel better about themselves and to be happier with others. But what if they've been using addiction to cover over their intrinsic shame? What if, now that they aren't drinking or drugging, they become flooded with all the feelings of worthlessness they've tried to hide from themselves? Many people recovering from addictions find themselves overwhelmed by a sense that they are no good, not good enough, and unlovable. Sometimes they end up feeling so bad about themselves that they literally want to die, just so they won't have to endure any more shame.

Obviously, it's not enough just to end an addiction. Not drinking, not gambling, "not" *anything* doesn't, by itself, heal shame. It merely creates a vacuum in people's lives that usually, sooner or later, will be filled with another problematic behavior. Unless they deal with their shame, many abstainers will return to their original addiction or find another, simply because they can no longer endure their own despair. Relapse to them becomes a way to survive—the only way they can see to survive.

Breaking the Shame/Addiction Connection

Here is what one woman, in her late sixties and in treatment for prescription drug dependency for the third time, told her treatment group: "My life would have been a lot better if only I had been a whole person all these years." This woman was expressing the terrible emptiness of addiction, the hollowed-out center of a person that no amount of alcohol or drugs can fill. Shame contributes to this emptiness because deeply shamed persons cannot accept themselves as they are. Shame drives people away from themselves and toward anything that might keep them from falling into their own personal black hole. Addictive and compulsive behaviors may mask this hole in the self, but they cannot heal it. Indeed, these behaviors usually increase the size of the hole over time and make the addict even more desperate to avoid it.

Shame-driven addicts face a difficult dilemma. They must quit their addictive behaviors to have any chance at a normal life. But when they try to stop, they risk being overwhelmed with their shame and emptiness. That pain may lead to relapse, as noted above. But every relapse only increases their shame, specifically the belief that they are failures. So, while shame undermines sobriety and causes relapse, relapse in turn increases shame and addiction.

Addictions are certainly difficult to end. We don't pretend to have all the answers in this small book. But we do believe that it is possible successfully to challenge the shame/addiction spiral. People wanting to break their personal shame/addiction connection can begin to do so by following these steps:

1. *Notice how your addictive behavior has helped you escape feelings of shame.* Remember that the shame/addiction spiral begins when people try to escape their bad thoughts about themselves. Those five negative judgments: I'm no good, I'm not good enough, I don't belong, I'm unlovable, and I should not exist—can feel intolerable when they keep nagging, shouting, and screaming in your mind. No wonder people try to get away from them. Alcohol, drugs, eating, gambling, sex, and other addictions are all temporary escapes from those thoughts.

   If this material applies to you, then you need to ask yourself one basic question: "What negative thoughts about myself was I thinking and feeling right before I last gave in to my addiction?" Were you thinking, perhaps, that there was something wrong with you (you were no good), or that you would never be a success (not good enough), or that your partner was about to throw you out (you don't belong), or that nobody likes you (unlovable), or even that you should die (you should not be). Or were you looking for anything that would help you avoid these kinds of thoughts? These shameful thoughts and fears are the fuel for many addictions. The first thing you need to do, then, is to identify those thoughts that most frequently trigger your escape into addictive behaviors.

2. *Now notice how your addictive behaviors have actually increased your shame.* There are two main ways that addictive behaviors increase shame. First are the negative consequences that all too quickly start piling up: withdrawal symptoms, mental

anguish, guilt, damaged or lost relationships, financial problems, deteriorating health, impaired job performance, worried family members, and maybe trouble with the law. These terrible consequences lead to even poorer self-esteem. They also provide reasons to become even more addicted. Negative consequences increase shame.

The second way that addiction increases shame is through loss of control. People defend against admitting they've lost control of their own lives. They use denial ("Hey, I don't have a marijuana problem") and minimization ("Okay, I do, but it's just a little one") so they don't have to face that particularly devastating reality. But loss of control is a part of all addictive and compulsive patterns. Addicts no longer have very many choices about what they can and cannot do. When their addiction orders them to jump they can only ask "how high?" and sometimes they don't even have a say in that matter. Loss of control is intrinsically shaming. It makes people feel defective, inept, worthless, and stupid.

It's critical for you to recognize how your addiction has caused you to lose control over your life and how that loss of control has added to your shame. That's the only way you can get past your own defenses of denial and minimization to find the truth.

Warning: It may be quite painful to see how you've lost control of your own life. So be careful. You may need to have people you trust around who you can talk with about this subject. At any rate, don't let discovering how you have been out of control just be another excuse to pursue your addiction. Learning how you've lost control, after all, might very well be the first step in getting some back.

3. *You must come to believe that shame is not an enemy.* A fundamental misbelief lies at the core of the shame/addiction spiral. This misbelief is the idea that shame is an enemy that wants to attack or even destroy you. Thinking that shame is an enemy leads people to flee it any way they can. The fear of shame sets the stage for addiction when people discover that addictive or compulsive behavior helps them gain a little distance from their shame.

At worst, some addicted persons have a gut fear that their shame could kill them. Their shame would be too terrible to endure. There is a seldom used word in the English language that best describes this feeling. That word is "mortification: a feeling of humiliation or shame, as through some injury to one's pride or self-respect" (*Random House Unabridged Dictionary*, Second Edition, 1993). The Latin root for *mortify* means "death" or "to put to death." And death is exactly what extreme shame feels like—a kind of psychological death of the soul. Some persons, then, run from their shame as if fleeing their own death. They truly fear that their shame would kill them, perhaps by their own hand.

Addiction represents a flight from shame. Paradoxically, the addiction itself might prove fatal both to body and mind. But it isn't designed for that purpose. Rather, addiction becomes a way to avoid the shame monster inside that constantly threatens self-annihilation.

But shame is not a monster. It isn't even a real enemy. Shame is merely an emotion, something natural and useful in moderation. Shame itself does not have the power to kill. Indeed, the fear of shame is more damaging than shame itself to many addicts. It's the dread of shame that drives people into addiction more than the shame itself. And it is fear of shame that keeps some people addicted.

To break the shame/addiction connection, then, you must develop the courage to face your shame. You must know deep inside that you will survive that encounter. You don't necessarily have to make friends with your shame, but you do need to become well enough acquainted with it so you don't have to live in terror. The most important idea to remember as you do this is: "My shame is part of me. It is only a feeling. I can handle meeting my shame."

4. *Make a commitment and take action.* All the insight in the world won't stop you from drinking, drugging, or any other addiction. At some point you'll need to take action. Basically, you'll need to make a commitment to cease behaviors that feed the shame/addiction spiral. You may call that decision by whatever name that fits best for you: abstinence, sobriety, sanity, control, acceptance of powerlessness, and so on. Whatever you call it, you'll need to follow through by stopping whatever actions keep bringing you shame.

But stopping shame-producing actions is just a beginning. You'll also need to start or increase activities that bring you a feeling of pride (see chapter 2, "What Is the Opposite of Shame"). Otherwise, your shame will hover constantly at the edges of your awareness, waiting to drag you back into your addiction. Of course, you'll probably have plenty of time to undertake these pride-enhancing activities. It's amazing what people have time and energy for once they take back control of their lives.

The goal is simply to feel good about yourself. That won't happen by luck or accident, though. Nor will it occur just because you aren't actively practicing an addiction. You'll need to develop a daily regime of positive health and ego-improving behaviors. Then, indeed, your life will get better and you'll feel a real sense of self-respect.

5. *Get help, get support.* Shame often drives people into isolation. But few people really heal very much while stuck deep inside their protective caves. You'll greatly increase your chance for long-term health and lessen the possibility of relapse by connecting with others.

We certainly recommend Alcoholics Anonymous, Narcotics Anonymous, Alanon, and other self-help groups. These groups can be particularly useful for people who thought they were alone in their pain and misery. People in good self-help groups don't just sit around and talk about their addictions, by the way. They actively help each other gain pride, self-respect, and competence at the same time they help each other stay sane and sober.

Not everybody wants to join these groups, though. If you don't, then it's important that you come up with a viable alternative. Who will you talk with when you're feeling ashamed? Who will you allow to become part of your support network? Your support network may be composed of friends, family, professional counselors, buddies at work, and other recovering people. Just remember that shame feeds on isolation. Addicts who say they will handle their shame all by themselves are exactly the persons more likely to wind up handling their shame with a bottle, gambling ticket, or line of cocaine.

Shame is diminished in the presence of caring, nonshaming friends. It's up to you to find these people and make them a regular part of your life.

Exercises

1. Fears of abandonment may play a large part in your addiction. The person who is afraid of abandonment has often actually experienced abandonment or strong and regular threats of it. This can take the form of someone dying, of having to leave the nuclear

family (even a temporarily absence can affect a child), of having experiences of neglect or rejection, or of having been threatened with being abandoned.

Take a few minutes and list the experiences of abandonment or threats of abandonment that have occurred in your life. How have these experiences affected you? Is there an activity in your life that could be addictive? If so, can you see that activity as a way that you have learned to abandon yourself rather than address any emotional pain or uncertainty?

2. You may use addictions to fill a sense of emptiness in your self or your life. There are many images of emptiness that are commonly used. Some examples are:

  · running on empty;
  · being like a black hole;
  · feeling hollow inside;
  · being an empty shell;
  · being invisible;
  · being a big zero;
  · being a balloon full of hot air;
  · being always spaced out;
  · having no center;
  · being a robot;
  · being bored with yourself.

These and other images of emptiness often represent loneliness, hurt, and grief too painful to keep in everyday awareness—despair and hopelessness that you have neutralized. Which of these images are most relevant to you, and why?

Do you have a compulsive or addictive behavior in your life that you use to fill your emptiness? Does it really fill you up?

Remember that even an empty glass has oxygen in it, and that that is what gives us life. Breathe deeply, and you will be amazed at what you can find in your emptiness. Take a little time and think about this.

3. There is a relationship between addiction and the need for finding a positive identity. Some believe that addiction is part of a misguided search for the spiritual. Certainly identity has a spiritual component to it. Each person is unique. There are times when shame over a past choice, a current trait, or extra criticism is difficult to face. Identity is having the courage to face the issue anyway, so you can know more fully who you are.

Take the letters of your name and make a positive acronym from it. An acronym is a set of words starting with the letters in another word, such as:

R = Responsible	**W** = Willing
O = On the ball	**I** = Introverted
G = Grateful	**L** = Loving
E = Enthusiastic	**C** = Creative
R = Riddle	**O** = Overcoming

In doing this, you have both chosen and become aware of qualities that are an important part of your identity.

11

Shame and Self-Hatred

Shame, Badness, and Five Types of Self-Hatred

Humans seem to be the planet's experts on self-destructive behavior. People have an incredible ability to attack themselves. They do so by ignoring their needs, calling themselves nasty names, feeling guilty when they've done nothing wrong, starving their bodies, cutting and burning themselves, and sometimes even trying to take their own lives. The basic question about this behavior that is so simple but so hard to answer is "Why?" Why do people hurt themselves physically and emotionally? Our suggestion is that self-destructive behavior is frequently the result of a blend of chronic shame with strong anger.

Shame comes first. Shame always makes people feel bad about themselves. For most people this sense of deficiency is temporary and limited to some immediate defect or problem. "True, I just made a fool out of myself and I feel ridiculous, but pretty soon I'll get over it." But sometimes, when shame has become chronic, that sense of badness feels permanent. That's when people believe they are irredeemably bad, beyond forgiveness or repair. They are broken and should be thrown away. If nobody else will do the rejecting, they will take care of the job themselves. The result is that deeply shamed people throw themselves away: "I don't like me. I don't want to be near me. I would never want to have myself for a friend." People with chronic shame, in other words, treat their own beings with disdain.

Strong anger is the second ingredient that produces self-hatred. While shame tends to depress and weaken, anger provides the energy to attack. Thus, the more angry people are with themselves the more likely they are to engage in self-destructive activity. If shame is the judge, declaring one's self to be bad and in need of punishment, then anger is the punisher. Judges don't always decide upon one single punishment, however. Indeed, in the matter of shame-based self-destructiveness, there are at least five possible sentences.

1. **Neglect.** You must ignore the self. Do not attend to your wants or needs.

2. **Blame.** You must blame yourself for whatever bad things happen and you must find fault with everything you do.

3. **Defeat.** You must make sure you fail. You don't deserve any success or goodness.

4. **Attack.** You must hurt yourself physically and emotionally. You must feel pain and suffering because of your badness.

5. **Death.** You must kill yourself because you are so terrible.

Self-destructiveness is the name we give these five combinations of shame and anger. But self-hatred is the name for the underlying condition. It is when people feel self-hatred that they become self-destructive. Self-haters, then, have come to believe they are so shameful that they must harm themselves in active or passive ways. Sometimes they think that acts of self-harm will redeem them. They hope they can reduce or eliminate their shame by purging it from their bodies through self-punishment. It's this kind of thinking that drives some bulimics to vomit (Kaufman 1996) as they try almost literally to eject their shame in a sort of purification ritual. Other self-haters, though, are less hopeful. They hurt their bodies and call themselves names only because they believe they so richly deserve to be punished. Their physical wounds signify their mental failures just as their scars indicate that their bodies may survive but will never again be whole.

The self-hatred that drives self-destructive behavior takes many forms. Some are obvious, some subtle. Some are seemingly minor, others life threatening. The central reality, though, no matter the shape or size of the actions, is that chronic shame can lead people to treat themselves as an enemy.

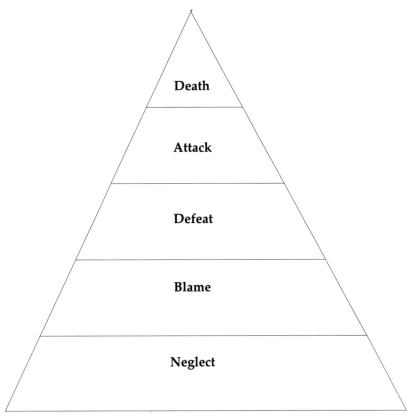

Figure 2.   SELF-DESTRUCTIVE PYRAMID

The Self-Hatred Pyramid

Self-hatred occurs in the five forms mentioned before: self-neglect, blame, defeat, attack, and death. The distribution of self-destructive behavior among these types is pyramidal, as you can see in the illustration of the Self-Hatred Pyramid. By far, the greatest number of self-destructive events are relatively minor acts involving neglect and blame. Self-defeat is less frequent but often quite harmful. Self-attack is relatively rare but damaging. Finally, attempts to take one's life are an extreme form of self-hatred and obviously the most dangerous. Thus, the frequency of self-destructive behaviors goes down as their strength and potential lethality climbs.

Most people have some familiarity with the self-destruction pyramid. For example, almost everybody will occasionally neglect their needs or say or think something nasty about themselves. Even self-defeat is far from rare if you think of it as a failure to thrive because people simply don't believe they are worthy of success. Occasional experiences like this with self-destructive shame, however, don't mean that people are shame bound. But the higher steps of the pyramid, self-attack and suicidality, are visited more frequently by people with excessively strong and tenacious feelings of shame (and by those suffering from severe depression, which may or may not be connected with shame).

We will describe the five types of self-destructive behavior in greater detail during the rest of this chapter, along with suggestions about how to change these behaviors.

Self-Neglect

Sally is a great caretaker. She gives of herself generously, indeed far too generously. That's why she's here volunteering at the hospital gift store for the fourth Saturday in a row. The manager just couldn't find anyone else again so she begged her old reliable, Sally, to come in. True, Sally had planned to watch her college basketball team play that day, but she soon agreed to cancel her date. Nor is this an unfamiliar scene. Sally regularly sets aside her own wants and needs in favor of others. She's so busy helping people out that she doesn't usually even take time to visit the doctor, go shopping, or have fun.

Does Sally secretly resent all this? Not at all. But she does have a secret, something she hides from everyone—her shame. Sally thinks of herself as worse than others, as somehow unworthy of being loved for her own sake. That's why she spends so much time caring for others. She hopes by doing so that people will at least tolerate her existence. She believes that other people think something like this: "Oh, well, Sally's not much, but we'll put up with her as long as she takes care of us." So Sally neglects herself partly to punish herself for being so worthless and partly to keep from being rejected.

Self-neglect is the hidden dimension of self-hatred. People who are self-neglectful simply ignore their own beings. This may reflect their early experiences. Many self-neglecters remember childhoods in which they felt they could never get their parents' attention. They eventually concluded that there must be something wrong with them, something that made them unworthy of attention. They also decided that, if they were so bad that even their parents wouldn't attend to them then they certainly weren't worthy of their own attention, either. They learned to notice everybody but themselves, to attend to everyone but themselves, to care about everybody but themselves. Their punishment for being shameful, then, is a kind of exile of the soul. They banish their own beings to a far-off corner of their mind so that they can concentrate on others. They reject themselves in order to keep from being rejected.

Sally, like many shame-wracked caregivers, may eventually collapse from sheer exhaustion. She can't regulate her caregiving very well because any act of self-caring is forbidden. She simply cannot allow herself to notice what she wants or desires, much less get her basic needs met. That would be selfish. People wouldn't want her around if she started taking care of herself. So the Sallys of this world work until they drop, rest just long enough to get some strength back, and then rush out to help others all over again. For them, self-neglect has become a way of life.

Self-neglect can be challenged, however. Here's how:

Listen for Your Inner Self-Nurturer

There's a self-nurturing voice inside everybody. That voice says something like this: "Honey, dear, it's really all right to take care of yourself. It's okay to know what you need. It's fine to take some time caring for yourself." Self-neglecters have this voice, just like everybody else. They simply have to learn to listen for it. That means quieting your shame and fear of rejection for a while. If you can do that, even for a few minutes at a time, you'll be able to hear your self-nurturing voice speaking to you from deep inside your being. You might only hear a whisper at first, but that voice will get louder as you pay more attention to it.

Commit to Self-Care

Just hearing that voice isn't enough. You'll actually have to start taking its advice. So, for instance, if your nurturing voice says you need to make a dentist appointment, then you need to make that appointment. To do so, though, you'll have to commute your self-imposed life sentence of self-neglect. That means forgiving yourself for your imagined or actual deficiencies. It means making a commitment to treat yourself as kindly as you treat others. It also means you'll have to face head on your beliefs that you are unimportant to others and that people will certainly reject you if you ask anything for yourself.

Actually Take Better Care of Yourself

Don't just make that dental appointment. Keep it. But there's more to ending self-neglect than just basic body maintenance. You'll also need to attend to your wishes, wants, and desires. So let yourself dream. What would you really like to do, see, experience, own? Make yourself a wish list. Then turn it into a *want* list by actually following through to get some of those wishes met. Keep listening to your inner nurturer so that it gradually becomes a part of you that you take pride in.

Self-Blame

"No matter what I do, it's never enough. I keep telling myself that I could have done better, I should have done more. Everybody else seems happy with me. It's me, not them, who's never satisfied. I feel like I've got somebody inside me who's always pointing out my shortcomings."

We call this voice the "internalized critic." Depending on events, the critic can sound angry ("You idiot!"), disgusted ("You're pathetic"), disappointed ("Is that all?"), or contemptuous ("You fool!"). Your critic may whisper disquieting messages in your ear when you're trying to think or talk. It may interrupt your privacy or even wake you up with a sudden curse or insult. Your internalized critic may speak only once in a while or haunt your life like a ghost that won't disappear. Most frequently, the critic talks in the same voice as your regular thoughts. Occasionally, though, the voice may sound as if someone else has snuck into your brain just to call you names. That someone may be recognizable: a parent, your spouse, your boss, in which case they may be saying things those people actually said to you in the past. Alternatively, the voice may not belong to you or to any specific other person. But whether the voice sounds like your own or another's, and whether it speaks in whispers or shouts, the message is all too clear: You've blown it again and you'll never do things right.

Self-blamers live life as if they were on trial. They themselves act as the district attorney preparing the indictment. Then they appoint a prosecutor who is always the best in town. And then they put a hanging judge on the bench. Finally, they hire the weakest, poorest excuse for a lawyer as their defender, someone who really thinks their client is guilty anyhow, so why bother fighting? The only plea bargain these inept attorneys can cut to save your life is by agreeing to a sentence of perpetual shame.

But of what exactly are self-blamers accusing themselves? That they aren't good enough, of course. That they've fallen short, could have done better, made a mistake, that they are thoughtless, selfish, greedy, and fatally flawed.

What should the punishment be if found guilty of these crimes? First, to feel overwhelmingly shameful. Second, to be cast out from society because you don't really belong in your family, career, and so on. Third, to become convinced that you will never be good enough, that you've been given a life sentence for your failures.

It would be bad enough if there were only one trial. But self-blamers keep preparing one indictment after another. They constantly scan the content of their own lives for signs of weakness or defectiveness. Since nobody's perfect, they always find such evidence. Then it's back to court.

Self-blamers have a distorted sense of self. They relate only to their shame, seldom noticing the things they do right or the positive aspects of their lives. It's like they've aimed a camera at themselves in a way that puts their flaws in perfect focus while everything else is fuzzy. Concentrating on what is wrong with them, they seem unable to forgive themselves for being human and making mistakes. They have abandoned their whole selves because they can't take in their own goodness.

Self-blaming can't just be stopped overnight. That inner critical voice doesn't simply get tired and go away. However, it's possible to balance the scales over time, first by developing an inner praising voice that speaks alongside your critic, and eventually by learning how to accept both your strengths and weaknesses as part of the human condition.

Self-blamers are indeed guilty. But the crime they're guilty of is being human. The way through self-blame is not to punish but to understand and accept that all human beings are flawed.

Self-Defeat

"I'm an expert at ripping failure from the jaws of success. For instance, I lost a college scholarship because I never mailed back the acceptance letter. Then I backed out of marriage to someone I know I loved. Just last month, I dropped out of a manager-training program even though I had perfect grades. Why do I do that?"

Self-defeaters are people who regularly fail to accomplish things they are actually able to do. Often that means failing at important aspects of life (career, relationships). Perhaps even more frequently, self-defeat shows up when people do less well than expected at important tasks. But why does this happen? Self-defeaters fail for two main reasons: first, because they think they don't deserve to succeed; second, because they fear they will be rejected if they are too successful.

First comes the belief they are unworthy of success. Self-directed shame and anger keep people from believing in their own competence, and so they botch any tasks, plans, or programs that might bring them success. Nor do they consider themselves worthy of love, kindness, or affection. That leads them to undermine their personal relationships as well.

Many self-defeaters are self-saboteurs, sneakily destroying their very own attempts at success. These saboteurs practice passive aggression against themselves (for a more detailed description of passive aggression, see our chapter on "sneaky" anger in *Letting Go of Anger* 1995). Self-saboteurs frustrate the part of their own beings that strive toward competence and worthiness. They fail quietly by not doing things they are perfectly capable of doing. But true passive aggressors do absolutely nothing in an attempt to frustrate people they think are attempting to control them. Passive-aggressive self-saboteurs may not consciously realize they're full of shame and anger. It is only in their consistent history of failure and under-achievement that these elements of their personality are revealed.

On the other hand, some self-defeaters are fully aware of their plight. Every time they near success, the volume of the shaming voices in their heads goes way up. All they can think of is how bad they are. Their shame expects them to screw things up. It demands they fail. And so they fail, validating their unworthiness once again.

The second major cause for self-defeating behavior is fear of rejection. True, self-defeaters punish themselves by failing. But they may also feel relieved when they fail because then nobody will be threatened by their success. Indeed, the cause of self-defeating behavior for some people is a strong belief that others would be unhappy or envious of their success. They think that it's better to fail or to limit their success than to risk rejection from an envious parent, sibling, schoolmate, colleague, or boss. They may or may not remember specific incidents when people reacted negatively to their achievements. Regardless, they feel safer and more like they belong when they hide their abilities from others. To them, standing out means standing apart. Standing apart is dangerous and shameful and so must be avoided at all cost. They choose to punish themselves through self-defeating behaviors because of their fear of rejection.

To undo self-defeating behavior, both major causes must be challenged. Let's begin with the fear of rejection because of accomplishment. It's important here to ask yourself how this fear developed. Were there actual incidents where people criticized, punished, or ignored you because of something you did well? When did you decide it was safer to limit your accomplishments than to risk rejection? Just as importantly as the past, though, is this question: How dangerous would it be for you to succeed now? Who would be happy for you? Who would celebrate your achievements? Who might be unhappy or envious? What other ways could you handle other people's disapproval of your success other than failing or underachieving? Once you answer all these questions, you'll be in a better position to decide how much the fear of rejection should dominate your life at this time.

But what about that personal conviction that you aren't worthy of success? How can you combat the shame and doubt that undermines all your positive effort? Only by steadily working to improve your self-concept. You must speak quietly but firmly to your excessive shame, refusing to let it keep controlling you. Furthermore, you need to make a personal commitment to quit punishing yourself through failure. But simply promising yourself to do better isn't enough. You'll also need to review how, when, and where your self-defeating patterns kick in. You'll probably notice that your failures follow definite sequences that are almost like rituals. The closer you get to the time you normally sabotage yourself, the more pressure you'll feel to fail. That's when you'll most need to get support from your true friends to deal with your success anxiety. You'll also need to be creative and alert, because breaking failure rituals calls for continued conscious thoughtfulness.

Self-Attack

"I hurt myself because I hate myself. I call myself names like 'slut' and 'whore.' But even that's not enough. I sometimes feel a need to punish my body, to make myself hurt on the outside as much as I hurt on the inside. That's when I cut or burn myself."

Self-attack is probably more common than usually recognized. Who hasn't, from time to time, called themselves nasty names, perhaps in response to a sudden failure or wave of shame? How many people at least once in a while literally pull their hair, smack their heads, or perhaps get so angry with themselves that they smash their fists into a wall in an act of self-punishment? "Idiot!" you might say to yourself, as you suddenly lash out against yourself. That sudden punishment may alleviate your feelings of shame. Of course, it might also increase those feelings when you realize you've just damaged your own body. But for most people these angry shame attacks against the self are infrequent and limited in intensity. That's not always true, however. Self-attack can become a regular, even dominant, part of some people's lives.

When shame and anger combine at the strongest levels, it's often not enough merely to underachieve or fail. That kind of self-defeating behavior is far too passive for persons who have come to hate and despise their very being. They think of themselves as unutterably vile, perhaps not all the time, but pretty regularly. It's during these shame/rage episodes that they verbally attack their self-worthiness and sometimes physically assault their bodies. The message in their name calling, cutting, burning, head-slamming, and other acts of self-inflicted torture is that they *must suffer*. Their physical wounds also serve to display the inner torment of their existence, the excruciating pain of their being, by converting mental anguish into something very concrete and visible.

We do want to mention that the meaning of self-attacking behavior varies widely. Every individual has a unique message in their self-inflicted pain. Some of these messages have little to do with shame itself, so it's important to make no assumptions. But if you could hear the deeper meanings of their wounds, the core messages, you might find that many would be shame related: I hurt myself because I am bad; I hurt myself because I am ashamed and afraid; I hurt myself to feel anything at all (by people who have become numb to block their feelings of shame); I hurt myself to call your attention to my pain; I hurt myself to give reality to subjective pain; I humiliate myself in the same ways other people once humiliated me; I hurt myself to distract from my emotional pain; I hurt myself because I deserve to hurt; I hurt myself because I am so full of badness (Potter-Efron 1991; Wise 1990).

Sometimes, too, self-attackers turn their anger against others onto themselves. That happens when it's safer to attack yourself than others, especially when it would be emotionally or physically dangerous even to be assertive, much less actually to express anger out loud. This is the experience of many children and adults who are the victims of physical or sexual abuse. They must do something with their anger, but they dare not direct it at their abusers. Instead, they turn it inward, along with their shame about being too weak to stop the attacks. Sadly, this turning inward means that they eventually become their own abusers.

Self-attacking behavior is not meant to be fatal. As bad as it looks when someone physically harms their own body, these attacks aren't suicide attempts. They are punishments.

Can self-attackers learn to quit harming themselves? Yes, definitely. But self-attack is hard to break for three main reasons: each attack against the self increases shame and further lowers self-esteem; self-attack can become a habitual response to stress; during these episodes the brain may release morphine-like pain-killing chemicals that can become addictive. Nevertheless, change is possible. People aren't doomed to attack themselves mercilessly until they die. That's not the purpose nor meaning of existence.

Change begins by declaring a temporary moratorium on self-harming thoughts and behavior. That's a lot like declaring a truce between longtime warring enemies, such as the Northern Irish Catholics and Protestants or the Israelis and Palestinians. You know that, despite the truce, there will be still be a few random skirmishes and episodes, in this case occasional name calling and body harm. If unchecked, each violation of the truce could lead to all-out war again. But instead, wiser heads usually prevail at these times, reminding people that peace is what they really want.

The parties to this particular truce are the self-shaming parts of you that insist on perpetual punishment and the self-caring parts of you that keep trying to fight off the shamer. Declaring a truce gives time for both sides to begin a dialogue. Hopefully, the final result of this dialogue will be the conversion of chronic shame into positive self-worth most of the time, along with occasional periods of moderate and temporary shame.

The goal is to stop or minimize self-abusive behavior. Assertiveness training may be useful for this purpose since aggression against the self may be misdirected anger against others. Other avenues to explore are developing a support network of nonshaming people you can call instead of hurting yourself, and finding a therapist who will help understand the sources of the self-attacking messages. Positive imagery may also be valuable. Imagine, for example, that the judge who sentenced you to perpetual punishment has now retired from the bench. Perhaps it's time to replace that judge with a more merciful one who will finally let you go free. After all, haven't you been punished enough for whatever you've done or failed to do in the past? Isn't it time to leave your past pain and shame in order to enter a better present?

Death

"I'm a pitiful excuse for a human being. I'm crap. Nobody loves me and why should they? I'm not worth loving. It would be better for everybody if I were dead. I'd kill myself today, if I had the guts."

Suicidal thoughts and attempts might be caused by many factors. Most frequently people considering suicide are tremendously depressed and have lost hope that they could ever be happy. Sometimes one important problem can spur suicidality, as when a teen gets jilted or an adult is diagnosed with an eventually fatal disease. We believe particularly severe combinations of shame and anger also promote suicide. This combination produces people who think they are so worthless or bad that they must die.

"I should not exist" is the shame-filled thought that promotes suicide. Add enough anger to this shame and you have a person fully capable of ending their own life. They rage against their own beings, plotting methods to eliminate them. They may even treat their bodies as objects somehow removed from themselves, saying out loud or to themselves that "it" must die. They often feel doomed in their certainty that they should, must, and will die of their own hands. In addition, many shame-based suicidal people have an internalized annihilator within them. The voice of that annihilator insists they die. Nothing less than self-extermination will ever satisfy the annihilator within.

Suicidally shamed people are tormented by one idea: "I have failed the test." But exactly what test is this? Nothing less than the test of global worthiness: Am I good enough to be? Their answer is, "Absolutely not." Their punishment is death.

There is hope, though. People can challenge their own death wish. One way is to realize that life is not a test. There are no official standards for being "good enough." You can't fail that test because there *is* no test. Everybody is good enough. Comparisons are useless.

We believe that shame-based suicide can be prevented. In the short run, people have to remember that they are important to others. They will truly be missed if they kill themselves. They also need to get in touch with that part of themselves that fights their internalized annihilator. There is almost always a spark of life in people, no matter how suicidal they appear. That spark within, a person's self-preserver, values life itself. Furthermore, the self-preserver senses a great truth—that life itself is something to be treasured. This wisdom is expressed in one small sentence: "I am."

"I am" is the healing principle for people whose suicidality is shame driven. "I am" is a simple declarative statement. It comes with no qualifier, modifier, comparison, apology, or excuse. "I am" is a fact, not a judgment. It merely announces the obvious, that someone is alive. The reasons people live are known only to the universe. But the *fact* of life is indisputable. "I am" focuses people on the present, not the past or future.

Indeed, "I am" is the fundamental healing principle for everyone facing self-destructive shame at any level. It helps self-neglecters remember to take care of themselves, self-blamers to make fewer deprecating judgments, self-saboteurs quit undermining their own doings, self-attackers call a reprieve, and self-annihilators finally accept their own being. "I am" returns the self to the self.

Exercises

1. One of the most important projects for those who suffer from any degree of self-hatred is finding their self-nurturing voices. First of all, if you are a self-hating person, that self-nurturing voice has had to hide itself. Like a puppy who's been hit once too many times, that voice is going to stay behind the couch when you call it, rather than come out and get smacked again. So you'll have to go find it.

   One way to do that is to go to a thrift store and find a neglected or abandoned stuffed animal or a sturdy statue. Take this object home with you. It has been awhile since this object has been taken care of, so set it somewhere you'll notice it often and decide what it needs. Then give it what it needs, personally. If it needs warming up, take it out and sit with it in the sun. If it needs washing off, take it swimming with you when you go. If it needs a place where it can see clearly, take it to a window and let it look out for a while. If it needs cheering up, tell it knock-knock jokes (playing both parts), or put on a funny movie and let it watch. The more you take care of it, and the more you listen to its voice and give it what it needs, the more the voice will tell you. If you continue to care for it, it will become, once again, your own voice.

2. It is hope that puts the cracks in self-hate and begins the process of self-redemption. When self-hate is not a result of depression, it's often the result of having done something that feels so shameful that you believe that you can never rejoin humanity. A man came to us to say that he was desperate. He had recovered from a crack addiction, gone to school, and become a counselor for other crack addicts. He had thought that he could count on himself to be honest and reliable and to do the right thing. But he hadn't. Even though he was happy in his new marriage with his wife and daughter, he had cheated on his wife. She had found out, and they had left him. While he wanted to try to repair his marriage, he was afraid. He feared he would do something dishonest and hurt his wife or family again. He no longer trusted himself or the rightness of anything he did, and he hated himself for having failed at being a man of conscience. We sent him out to visit a place where there are many big, old trees. Although all the trees are living, towering over the earth, all have big holes in them, or broken branches.

Some have had metal supports put in them. The damage is apparent. We asked him to sit down and have a dialogue with one of those trees, and he did. Later, he returned and told us that he had sat there for an hour, and that he now understood himself a little better. He no longer hated himself. He realized, he said, that every being gets damaged by life in some way, and he had seen how those trees grew around their damage and went right on. He could see that, in spite of the problems they had encountered in their growing, they were still strong and beautiful. "And," he said, "if I work hard at continuing to grow, I can be that way too."

Go for a walk and find something that speaks gently to you. Avoid those things that you know will make your self-hate worse, and focus on something you haven't noticed before, something that catches your attention. Your right brain will help you do this, so don't worry about doing it incorrectly. When you find that thing that calls to you and can speak gently, take some time with it. Ask what it has to teach you about your life, and if it can give you any advice on feeling better about yourself.

3. Self-hate is a little like sitting in a pile of manure. It stinks. Even good, clean manure is unhealthy. It gets smeared all over, until you can't stand yourself. So, getting rid of that self-hate will take some considerable cleansing. We're talking about an emotional process here, a letting go of that self-hate. This can be done in imagination, or for real, in the shower. Here is how it goes. Imagine you are standing in a shower or under a waterfall. The water rushing down over you is light pastel of every color. As it curls around you and runs down your body, it washes any harsher or darker colors around you away. You can see them swirling around and going down the drain. This pastel falling of water reaches all around you, out to about two feet on every side. The darker colors simply melt away and swirl down the drain. If there is a spot where they cling, put that part of your body or aura right in the flow of water (real or imaginary). There is nothing stronger than light, and the pastel light will scrub away any gunk you have collected.

Do this at least once a day, until you find it a clear and easy visualization that you can turn to instead of turning against yourself.

Afterword

It's never easy to sum up a book in a few paragraphs. There is simply so much content to sort through. But the main point we'd like to emphasize isn't about the specifics of shame and rage or addiction or body image. Rather, we want to end by stressing once again the positive possibilities that can, and we hope did, emerge from your reading and thinking about shame.

First, investigating your shame pushed shame out of the shadows and into daylight. We mentioned in the preface that shame is the werewolf of emotions because it thrives in dark. Really working on your shame issues gives you more, and shame less, control of your life.

Second, dealing with your shame may have pointed you toward some very positive goals. Anyone who feels shame is also capable of feeling dignity, honor, wholeness, integrity, and so on. You can't pick up the coin of shame without also having the coin of healthy pride in your hand.

Third, your shame always says something about your being. Reading about shame might have helped you discover who you are in a deep, meaningful way.

Finally, we hope that your reading this book has helped you travel in the direction of self-love and self-respect. That was the main reason for writing it.

References

Alcoholics Anonymous. 1976. *Big Book*. New York: A.A. World Services.

Bandura, Alfred. 1997. *Self-Efficacy: The Exercise of Control*. New York: W.H. Freeman and Company.

Bradshaw, John. 1988. *Healing The Shame That Binds You*. Deerfield Beach, Fl.: Health Communications, Inc.

Buber, Martin. 1958. *I and Thou* (2nd edition). New York: Scribner's.

Cameron, Julia. 1992. *The Artist's Way: A Spiritual Path to Higher Creativity*. Los Angeles: J.P. Tarcher/Perigree.

Capacchione, Lucia. 1979. *The Creative Journal*. Athens, Ohio: Swallow Press.

Goldberg, Natalie. 1998. *Writing Down the Bones*. New York: Shambala Publications.

Kaufman, Gershen. 1996. *The Psychology of Shame* (2nd edition). New York: Springer.

Lewis, Michael. 1992. *Shame: The Exposed Self*. New York: Free Press.

Marquez, Gabriel Garcia. 1988. *Love in the Time of Cholera*. New York: Knopf.

Morrison, Andrew. 1989. *Shame: The Underside of Narcissism*. Hillsdale, New Jersey: The Analytic Press.

Piers, G. and M.B. Singer. 1953. *Shame and Guilt*. New York: Norton.

Potter-Efron, Ronald. 1989. *Shame, Guilt and Alcoholism.* New York: Haworth.

———. 1994. *Angry All The Time*. Oakland, Cal.: New Harbinger Publications.

———. 1998. *Being, Belonging, Doing: Balancing Your Three Greatest Needs*. Oakland, Cal.: New Harbinger Publications.

Potter-Efron, Ronald and Patricia. 1989a. *I Deserve Respect*. Center City, Mn.: Hazelden Educational Materials.

———. 1989b. *Letting Go of Shame*. Center City, Mn.: Hazelden Educational Materials.

———. 1991. *Anger, Alcoholism and Addiction*. New York: W.W. Norton.

———. 1995. *Letting Go of Anger*. Oakland, Cal.: New Harbinger Publications.

Random House Unabridged Dictionary (2nd Edition). 1993. New York: Random House.

Retzinger, Suzanne. 1991. *Violent Emotions: Shame and Rage in Marital Quarrels*. Newbury Park, Cal.: Sage Publications.

Roth, Geneen. 1991. *When Food Is Love*. New York: Dutton.

Schneider, Carl. 1977. *Shame, Exposure and Privacy*. Boston: Beacon Press.

Volavka, Jan. 1995. *Neurobiology of Violence*. Washington, D.C.: American Psychiatric Press, Inc.

Wise, Mary Louise. 1990. "Adult Self Injury As a Survival Response in Victim-Survivors of Childhood Abuse." In Ronald and Patricia Potter-Efron, eds., *Aggression, Family Violence and Chemical Dependency*. New York: Haworth.

MORE NEW HARBINGER TITLES

WORKING ANGER
Preventing and Resolving Conflict on the Job

Ron Potter-Efron offers a step-by-step program designed to help anyone who has had trouble dealing with their own anger or other people's anger at work.

Item WA $12.95

ANGRY ALL THE TIME
An Emergency Guide to Anger Control

Ron's emergency guide to changing anger-provoking thoughts, dealing with old resentments, asking for what you want without anger, and staying calm one day at a time.

Item ALL Paperback, $12.95

LETTING GO OF ANGER

Ron and Pat Potter-Efron help you recognize the ten destructive ways that people deal with anger and identify which anger styles may be undermining your personal and work relationships.

Item LET Paperback, $13.95

BEING, BELONGING, DOING
Balancing Your Three Greatest Needs

Ron's thoughtful self-discovery exercises help us reevaluate priorities and explore practical ways of keeping the crucial components of our lives integrated and in balance.

Item BBD Paperback, $10.95

THE SELF-FORGIVENESS HANDBOOK
A Practical and Empowering Guide

Guided exercises, refined over the years in therapist Thom Rutledge's practice and motivating workshops, guide you on the inner journey from self-criticism to self-compassion and inner strength.

Item FORG Paperback, $12.95

Call **toll-free 1-800-748-6273** to order. Have your Visa or Mastercard number ready. Or send a check for the titles you want to New Harbinger Publications, 5674 Shattuck Avenue, Oakland, CA 94609. Include $3.80 for the first book and 75¢ for each additional book to cover shipping and handling. (California residents please include appropriate sales tax.) Allow four to six weeks for delivery.

PRICES SUBJECT TO CHANGE WITHOUT NOTICE.

Some Other New Harbinger Self-Help Titles

The Self-Esteem Companion, $10.95

The Gay and Lesbian Self-Esteem Book, $13.95

Making the Big Move, $13.95

How to Survive and Thrive in an Empty Nest, $13.95

Living Well with a Hidden Disability, $15.95

Overcoming Repetitive Motion Injuries the Rossiter Way, $15.95

What to Tell the Kids About Your Divorce, $13.95

The Divorce Book, Second Edition, $15.95

Claiming Your Creative Self: True Stories from the Everyday Lives of Women, $15.95

Six Keys to Creating the Life You Desire, $19.95

Taking Control of TMJ, $13.95

What You Need to Know About Alzheimer's, $15.95

Winning Against Relapse: A Workbook of Action Plans for Recurring Health and Emotional Problems, $14.95

Facing 30: Women Talk About Constructing a Real Life and Other Scary Rites of Passage, $12.95

The Worry Control Workbook, $15.95

Wanting What You Have: A Self-Discovery Workbook, $18.95

When Perfect Isn't Good Enough: Strategies for Coping with Perfectionism, $13.95

Earning Your Own Respect: A Handbook of Personal Responsibility, $12.95

High on Stress: A Woman's Guide to Optimizing the Stress in Her Life, $13.95

Infidelity: A Survival Guide, $13.95

Stop Walking on Eggshells, $14.95

Consumer's Guide to Psychiatric Drugs, $16.95

The Fibromyalgia Advocate: Getting the Support You Need to Cope with Fibromyalgia and Myofascial Pain, $18.95

Healing Fear: New Approaches to Overcoming Anxiety, $16.95

Working Anger: Preventing and Resolving Conflict on the Job, $12.95

Sex Smart: How Your Childhood Shaped Your Sexual Life and What to Do About It, $14.95

You Can Free Yourself From Alcohol & Drugs, $13.95

Amongst Ourselves: A Self-Help Guide to Living with Dissociative Identity Disorder, $14.95

Healthy Living with Diabetes, $13.95

Dr. Carl Robinson's Basic Baby Care, $10.95

Better Boundaries: Owning and Treasuring Your Life, $13.95

Goodbye Good Girl, $12.95

Fibromyalgia & Chronic Myofascial Pain Syndrome, $19.95

The Depression Workbook: Living With Depression and Manic Depression, $17.95

Self-Esteem, Second Edition, $13.95

Angry All the Time: An Emergency Guide to Anger Control, $12.95

When Anger Hurts, $13.95

Perimenopause, $16.95

The Relaxation & Stress Reduction Workbook, Fourth Edition, $17.95

The Anxiety & Phobia Workbook, Second Edition, $18.95

I Can't Get Over It, A Handbook for Trauma Survivors, Second Edition, $16.95

Messages: The Communication Skills Workbook, Second Edition, $15.95

Thoughts & Feelings, Second Edition, $18.95

Depression: How It Happens, How It's Healed, $14.95

The Deadly Diet, Second Edition, $14.95

The Power of Two, $15.95

Living Without Depression & Manic Depression: A Workbook for Maintaining Mood Stability, $18.95

Couple Skills: Making Your Relationship Work, $14.95

Hypnosis for Change: A Manual of Proven Techniques, Third Edition, $15.95

Letting Go of Anger: The 10 Most Common Anger Styles and What to Do About Them, $12.95

Infidelity: A Survival Guide, $13.95

When Anger Hurts Your Kids, $12.95

Don't Take It Personally, $12.95

The Addiction Workbook, $17.95

It's Not OK Anymore, $13.95

Beyond Grief: A Guide for Recovering from the Death of a Loved One, $14.95

The Chemotherapy & Radiation Survival Guide, Second Edition, $14.95

An End to Panic: Breakthrough Techniques for Overcoming Panic Disorder, Second Edition, $18.95

Dying of Embarrassment: Help for Social Anxiety and Social Phobia, $13.95

The Endometriosis Survival Guide, $13.95

Grief's Courageous Journey, $12.95

Flying Without Fear, $13.95

Stepfamily Realities, $14.95

Coping With Schizophrenia: A Guide For Families, $15.95

Conquering Carpal Tunnel Syndrome and Other Repetitive Strain Injuries, $17.95

The Three Minute Meditator, Third Edition, $13.95

The Chronic Pain Control Workbook, Second Edition, $17.95

The Power of Focusing, $12.95

Living Without Procrastination, $12.95

Kid Cooperation: How to Stop Yelling, Nagging & Pleading and Get Kids to Cooperate, $13.95

Call **toll free, 1-800-748-6273**, or log on to our online bookstore at **www.newharbinger.com** to order. Have your Visa or Mastercard number ready. Or send a check for the titles you want to New Harbinger Publications, Inc., 5674 Shattuck Ave., Oakland, CA 94609. Include $3.80 for the first book and 75¢ for each additional book, to cover shipping and handling. (California residents please include appropriate sales tax.) Allow two to five weeks for delivery.

Prices subject to change without notice.